"In an ever-changing world, we are in desperate need of a never-changing standard and perspective that should govern our lives and guide our decisions. My good friend Jack Graham has given us a solid, biblically sound tool to encourage, inspire, and instruct us in how to have, keep, and expand a faith that lasts."

—Dr. Tony Evans, president, the Urban Alternative;
senior pastor, Oak Cliff Bible Fellowship

"I have known Jack Graham since our teenage years and can personally attest to the fact that every truth found within these pages has been beaten out of the anvil of his own faith experience. His character is beyond reproach, and his reputation is spotless. If you are in need of a fresh focus on your own faith, this is the place to begin the journey and to reignite!"

—O. S. Hawkins, PhD, author of the bestselling CODE series,
including *The Joshua Code* and *The Bible Code*

"My pastor, Pastor Jack Graham, is one of the most dynamic and inspirational leaders of faith of our time. *Reignite* is a book that will inspire you to reactivate your personal relationship with Christ. It is a must-read for all Christians who want to be on fire for Jesus Christ."

—Coach Todd Graham, head football coach,
University of Hawaii

"It's rare when the pastor of a megachurch opens the doors of his soul to candidly share a journey of faith that has elements of fear and doubt. Jack Graham does just that in *Reignite*, and as he describes his walk, we better understand our own."

—Mike Huckabee, host, *Huckabee*

"Jack Graham is a beloved pastor, respected teacher, and clear thinker. As you will see in this wonderful book, Jack is also a fellow struggler. None of us gets through life pain-free. But God uses men like Jack and messages like these to keep us strong."

—Max Lucado, teaching minister, Oak Hills Church

"Jack Graham has shown for decades he is a usable tool in the Lord's hands. He's a strong leader, powerful preacher, and good friend, but *Reignite* adds to the list . . . vulnerable shepherd. As he shares his own heartfelt journey, you will be encouraged. Let Dr. Graham lead you to reignite the flame of your heart."

—Gregg Matte, pastor, Houston's First Baptist Church

"It can be hard for strong, forceful leaders to admit weakness. Yet this book is a frank, heartfelt discussion about the challenge of overcoming personal despair to reignite passion and purpose. Jack owns the struggle, providing testimony that will comfort, encourage, challenge, and reignite your heart too."

—Dr. David H. McKinley, pastor-teacher,
Warren Baptist Church

"Pastor Jack Graham is one of the great spiritual leaders in our world. This book will help you. Read it all. Read it now."

—Reverend Johnnie Moore, president, the Congress of
Christian Leaders; founder, the KAIROS Company

"Reading this book was like sitting in Dr. Graham's home, listening to him share about the tough moments he's faced and the timely lessons he's learned. This book is a tremendous encouragement, personal and biblical just like its author—very open, very honest, very helpful. Thank you, Jack!"

—Robert J. Morgan, author and speaker

"My friend Jack Graham is one of the most vulnerable and humble leaders I have ever met. In *Reignite*, he shares his story of battling anxiety and depression and how returning to the fundamentals of our faith led him to healing. This book is a balm for every weary soul living in troubling times."

—Reverend Samuel Rodriguez, lead pastor, New Season; president, NHCLC; author, *You Are Next*; executive producer, *Breakthrough*

"If this highly effective leader, known for his call and drive, can fall into a pit of darkness, then all of us are susceptible. Jack's story of pushing back the invisible and being set ablaze by the love of the Creator is one every person must read and share with others."

—Dr. Jay Strack, president, Student Leadership University

"I've had the privilege to serve under the leadership of Dr. Jack Graham for the last twenty years and have witnessed firsthand him live out the message of this book. In *Reignite: Fresh Focus for an Enduring Faith*, Pastor Graham shares how the broken and burned-out can experience a renewed sense of purpose and hope in the midst of uncertainty and pain."

—Jarrett Stephens, teaching pastor, Prestonwood Baptist Church; author, *The Always God: He Hasn't Changed and You Are Not Forgotten*

"What a read! *Reignite* will bring you to a place of greater faith, hope, and power! I greatly appreciated Pastor Jack Graham's life transparency, which is relational and leads to practical direction that will lift you out of any difficult time or season in your life."

—Darryl Strawberry, four-time World Series Champion, eight-time All-Star, evangelist

REIGNITE

REIGNITE

FRESH FOCUS
FOR AN
ENDURING FAITH

JACK GRAHAM

© 2021 by Jack Graham

Published by Bethany House Publishers
11400 Hampshire Avenue South
Bloomington, Minnesota 55438
www.bethanyhouse.com

Bethany House Publishers is a division of
Baker Publishing Group, Grand Rapids, Michigan

Printed in the United States of America

Library of Congress Cataloging-in-Publication Data
Names: Graham, Jack, author.
Title: Reignite : fresh focus for an enduring faith / Jack Graham.
Description: Minneapolis, Minnesota : Bethany House Publishers, a division of Baker Publishing Group, 2021.
Identifiers: LCCN 2020042955 | ISBN 9780764236020 (cloth) | ISBN 9780764236037 (trade paperback) | ISBN 9781493427987 (ebook)
Subjects: LCSH: Christian life. | Faith. | Resilience (Personality trait)—Religious aspects—Christianity.
Classification: LCC BV4501.3 .G7333 2021 | DDC 248.4—dc23
LC record available at https://lccn.loc.gov/2020042955

Cover design by LOOK Design Studio

Author is represented by Wolgemuth & Associates.

21 22 23 24 25 26 27   7 6 5 4 3 2

Contents

Foreword

I'm going to begin with a disclaimer: Dr. Jack Graham is my pastor and my friend. I have had the joy and privilege of sitting under his ministry for many years and have watched the way he has navigated tough seasons and also seasons of great joy and celebration. There are few people on this planet for whom I have such deep respect as I do for Pastor Graham.

When I was offered the opportunity to share a few words, I was honored to do so, but what I didn't realize until I read the final words of *Reignite* is just how deeply this book would impact my own life and faith. In a world where the temptation exists to present only our best selves, Pastor Graham is disarmingly transparent. When Paul wrote to the church in Thessalonica, he left a template for ministry that not many are comfortable with: "*We loved you so much that we shared with you not only God's Good News but our own lives, too*" (1 Thessalonians 2:8 NLT).

In this book, Pastor Graham gives us that costly gift. You will read about one of the greatest challenges any human being can face, presented in a profoundly unvarnished, vulnerable way. Because he is willing to share the personal pain and struggle he has walked through, his call to each one of us to stand up, to look up, to press on is soaked in integrity.

As I was navigating one of the hardest seasons in my own life, my pastor was there as a compassionate, wise counselor who acknowledged the pain of life and yet pointed me toward Christ, the One who was wounded and scarred for us. I will be eternally grateful.

If 2020 has left you discouraged and weary, this book will truly reignite your faith. Not only that, but it will provide the road map you need to get all the way home. If you are struggling to know how to navigate the world we now live in, you will find a wise friend in these pages to cheer you on.

Dr. Graham reminds us of

- why we believe what we believe,
- how to trade damaging thought patterns for life-giving grace, and
- the joy that awaits every one of us who chooses to keep their eyes fixed on Christ.

There are many things in our world that are deeply troubling, but our God is still on the throne, and the greatest battle has already been won. Let's walk into this new season with a reignited faith in Christ that will bring hope to those who still walk in darkness. I believe this book will be life changing.

Sheila Walsh, author of *Praying Women*

Author's Note

Dark Days Begging for Light

Bringing this book into the world was anything but a breezy affair. There was a medical pandemic, and then a cultural one roared in, and as the days turned to weeks, and the weeks gave way to months, I found myself increasingly disoriented and dismayed: What did all of these changes mean for us as a society in the future?

This book will always live in my memory as my "COVID-19 book," an assembly of thoughts and ideas and convictions that made their way into our collective consciousness during what has arguably been the most unprecedented, unpredictable, and un-welcome era in modern history. And yet I've seen firsthand that despite the darkness that descends on us, envelops us, and leaves us perplexed and shaking our heads, shafts of light still doggedly break in.

Ten years ago, as I navigated (if poorly) an unexpected bout with severe anxiety and depression, the rope that I eventually used to climb out of the pit I'd fallen into was made of the very raw materials you'll encounter in the pages that follow—time spent with God's Word, time with God himself, and consistency in making the choices that compelled me to live beyond myself. And what I can tell you, having made it to the other side of that harrowing experience, is that regardless of the brokenness you have known or the pain points that remain tender still today, there is One who is perfectly and predictably suited to pick you up, to see you through, to make you whole. If you are downcast and depleted, or like me, disoriented and dismayed, may these chapters remind you that your faith can be reignited and your hope can be restored.

God longs to do this work in us.

We need only ask him to.

Jack Graham

November 2020

PART ONE

Fundamentals of Our Faith

1

Truth That Never Turns

Like a finely tuned engine, our brains are designed for only one
fuel—Truth. The Truth that comes from God. The Truth that per-
vades His creation. The Truth found in His perfect character and
infallible Word.

Robert Morgan, *Reclaiming the Lost Art
of Biblical Meditation*

But as for you, continue in what you have learned and have firmly
believed, knowing from whom you learned it and how from childhood you have been acquainted with the sacred writings, which are
able to make you wise for salvation through faith in Christ Jesus.
All Scripture is breathed out by God and profitable for teaching,
for reproof, for correction, and for training in righteousness, that
the man of God may be complete, equipped for every good work.

2 Timothy 3:14–17

Clearly, I had underestimated what the process would involve.
It was 2009—and springtime, no less, the quintessential season of newness and hope. And yet there I stood, on the edge of a
dark chasm, the ground crumbling beneath my feet.

My longtime doctor, Dr. Kenneth Cooper, founder of the Cooper Aerobics Center in Dallas, had been watching my PSA numbers for quite some time—the better part of four years, in fact—and was growing increasingly concerned. In healthy males, prostate-specific antigens are supposed to remain relatively few in quantity. Mine didn't register as "few."

"It's your prostate," Dr. Cooper had told me, early in the game. "Something's off . . . but let me do a biopsy before we get ahead of ourselves."

We did the biopsy in 2009. Dr. Cooper processed the results. And then I got the phone call nobody wants to get. "I'd like you to come in again, Jack," the good doctor said, which told me everything I needed to know. A doc doesn't need to see a patient to deliver favorable news. The diagnosis I received during that in-person visit was a sobering one: "Prostate cancer." And this for a guy who rarely catches a cold.

Back to that "process" I mentioned. Once I had the diagnosis, I asked about a treatment plan. Evidently, surgery would be required—the equivalent of a hysterectomy, I was told—but I was fine with that. We'd cut out the offending agent, in this case my prostate gland, I'd hang out at home for a bit, and then I'd get back to the people I loved serving, the congregation of Prestonwood Church.

But God had another plan.

My surgery took place on May 14, a Thursday, which was three weeks and two days before an important milestone in the life of our church. During our worship services on the weekend of June 6 and 7, we would be celebrating my twentieth anniversary as senior pastor of Prestonwood, and I figured that if I "rested hard" for ten days, I'd be in great shape again, just in time for that glorious event. What I couldn't have foreseen was that not only would I be basically crawling into the pulpit to receive my commendation that first weekend in June, but I also would be spending the next many months disoriented, deflated, and suffering a diagnosis that felt equally grave: anxiety.

Anxiety?

Me?

My reflexive reaction was to wave it off. *But I'm Jack Graham!* I thought, incredulous. Turns out anxiety didn't care who I was.

I experienced panic and fear during that season unlike anything I'd known before. I had prayed prior to my surgery, "Lord, don't let me flinch in the fire," but I had no idea the flames would be that high or that the burn would be that deep. In Proverbs 12:25, we read that "anxiety in a man's heart weighs him down," and that's exactly what happened to me. Anxiety gave way to depression, and suddenly I was in the fight of my life.

Dead Man Walking

In his brilliant book on all sorts of mental illnesses, *Caring for People God's Way*, American Association of Christian Counselors President Tim Clinton, a friend of mine who has more letters behind his name than almost anyone I know, named depression the "common cold of emotional disorders"[1] and wrote that while the potential causes of depression are still debatable—Is it caused by a poor diet? By a lack of exercise? By chemical imbalances in the brain? What role does lack of sleep play in a person's propensity to deal with depression? Can you overwork your way into this state?—what's not debatable are the symptoms that inevitably occur.

"For *Major Depressive Disorder* to be diagnosed," he said, "one or more major depressive episodes must have occurred. This means the depressed person must have experienced at least two weeks of depressed mood (or irritable mood in children or adolescents) or loss of interest or pleasure in almost all activities, together with a minimum of four other symptoms of depression . . . such as: (1) marked weight loss when not dieting, weight gain, or change in appetite; (2) insomnia or excessive sleep; (3) slowed movements or agitation; (4) decreased energy or fatigue; (5) feelings of worthlessness or inappropriate or excessive guilt; (6) indecisiveness or decreased ability to concentrate; and (7) recurrent thoughts of death or suicide."[2]

The way I would characterize my experience was that of a dead man walking—or crawling, as the case may be.

Hopelessness.

Sadness.

Helplessness.

Despair.

Numbness.

Listlessness.

Despondency.

Loss of appetite.

(That last one was most concerning to my family. Man, how I love to eat.)

And then there was the insomnia. The insomnia was the *worst*. I'm the type of person who regularly logs six or seven hours of restful sleep. Sure, maybe it's not the eight or nine hours I was once able to net, but if you're from my generation or older, then you understand how aging affects us all. (If you're younger than I am and can still sleep like that, then you should fall to your knees and thank God right this moment. Things won't always be this way.)

"For my days pass away like smoke," the psalmist wrote in Psalm 102:3–9, "and my bones burn like a furnace. My heart is struck down like grass and has withered; I forget to eat my bread. Because of my loud groaning my bones cling to my flesh. I am like a desert owl of the wilderness, like an owl of the waste places; I lie awake; I am like a lonely sparrow on the housetop. All the day my enemies taunt me; those who deride me use my name for a curse. For I eat ashes like bread and mingle tears with my drink." Were we to title the various entries in the book of Psalms, this one would be called simply "Depressed."

Because I was not sleeping much during that awful ordeal, I found other ways to occupy my nights. Such as fretting. Slipping into full-on panic attacks. Inviting in anxiety like it was an old friend and asking it to stay awhile. "We're not sure we caught it all," the surgeon had informed me after I'd awakened from the anesthesia. Every night, as I lay in bed wide awake, I pictured the cancer filling my body to overflowing, water in a balloon that one day would burst.

For many months I was exhausted all the time, which made life feel like a weighted slog through a pool of mud—taxing, inefficient, slow. Emotionally, in a slide that this buoyant guy had never once experienced, I also developed a certain disdain for happiness in all its forms. Life was hard. Very hard.

Recently I came across the reflections of a distance runner on a particularly awful marathon he had competed in. The temperature outside was blazing hot, and despite his love for and his vast experience with the activity, that day he just didn't "have it."

"At around twenty-three miles I start to hate everything," he said of the race. "Enough already! My energy has scraped bottom, and I don't want to run anymore. I feel like I'm driving a car on empty. . . . I'm dying of thirst but lack the strength to even drink water anymore. As these thoughts flit through my mind I gradually start to get angry. Angry at the sheep happily munching grass in an empty lot next to the road, angry at the photographer snapping photos from inside the van. The sound of the shutter grates on my nerves. Who needs this many sheep, anyway? But snapping the shutter is the photographer's job, just as chewing grass is the sheep's, so I don't have any right to complain. Still, the whole thing really bugs me to no end. My skin's starting to rise up in the little white heat blisters. This is getting ridiculous. What's *with* this heat, anyway?"[3]

My equivalent of being irritated by sheep happily munching grass happened when I no longer wanted to be around my four-year-old grandson, Ian. This was a real low point for me, because as my only grandchild at the time, Ian was the light of my life. And yet I distinctly recall being ill-equipped to match his energy, his optimism, his spark. I've never been one to become upset to the point of tears, but the day I made that realization, I sobbed. Shortly thereafter I placed a call to a Christian counselor whose number I had been given. I was certain that nothing and nobody could help me, but something inside of me at least had to try.

Emerging from the Pit

It would take me a full year and a surfeit of resources to get out of the pit I'd unwittingly slid into, and among those resources was *time*.

Time Heals (Some) Wounds

I'm not sure the adage about time healing all wounds has it right, but time does indeed help. The only problem with that reality is that I'm not exactly a patient man. I have about a fifteen-minute-long tolerance before something needs to *move*. I distinctly remember lying in bed on a workday, sequestered there in Deb's and my master bedroom, willing the clock to tick faster, all but begging time to hurry along. During those weeks and months, a whole slew of smart people told me it would take a year for me to recover from my setbacks, but did I believe them?

Uh, *no*.

Still, I tried to be a good patient and even agreed to a two-month sabbatical on the heels of that twentieth-anniversary celebration at the church. If time was what was needed, then I would give this thing plenty of time. Ironically, exactly two weeks before my prostate surgery, I'd released a book I'd been working on for the better part of a year. *Powering Up* it was titled, despite its author now living powered down.

The Life-Giving Power of Touch

Just as important as the resource of time to heal my mind, my heart, my life was the resource of *touch*. As much as I hated to

24

admit it, I was in a real mess that year. I needed support, encouragement, and care. Plenty of friends and family members called and texted and even stopped by from time to time, but in addition to those generous acts, I took the initiative too. My friend O. S. Hawkins has been like a brother to me since we met as teenagers at Sagamore Hill Baptist Church in east Fort Worth, under the mentorship of Pastor Fred Swank, a true hero of the faith. We were called into ministry at the same time, we served in the same states at the same times—Texas, then Oklahoma, then Florida, then back to Texas—and we remain the closest of friends to this day. Having him close by as I wrestled through that dark season was a balm. "Remember, Jack," he told me in the heat of my battle, "there has never been a sunset that wasn't followed by a sunrise. Joy comes in the morning. Just hang on."

How I needed that simple, straightforward reminder. "Bear one another's burdens," Galatians 6:2 says, "and so fulfil the law of Christ." What a relief it was to have so many lovers of God agree to bear my burden with me. "Weeping may tarry for the night," Psalm 30:5 says, "but joy comes with the morning." Yes, the morning would come again.

Giving Thanks to God

And then there was the practice of *thanksgiving*. Each day, even on the days when I could barely string two coherent thoughts together, I would force myself to write down something I was grateful for. My goal was three things, though on some days there would be only one. Still, I held fast to that one thing, being sure to say "thank you" every day. I once heard that a negative attitude is like a flat tire; until you fix it, you're not going anywhere. I knew that was true for me then.

Study after study has confirmed that the moment you choose to express gratitude, your brain begins to change. Because the brain can only focus on one thing at a time, and because the brain has a distinct confirmation bias when you ask it to focus on something positive—say, something for which you're grateful—it goes in search of *more* things to be grateful for and won't stop until you tell it to. Thanksgiving begets thanksgiving until eventually all this positivity has an incontestable medicinal effect. It is the healthiest of all emotions.

The late Ed Dobson, who pastored in Grand Rapids, Michigan, was diagnosed with ALS—Lou Gehrig's disease—in 2000 and died fifteen years later from the muscle degeneration caused by the horrific disease. Three years before his death, in his book *Seeing through the Fog*, he noted his current gratitude list as something of a prayer. "Lord, thank you that I can still go to the bathroom by myself," he wrote. "Lord, thank you that I can still brush my teeth. Lord, thank you that I can still take a shower. Lord, thank you that I can still use a towel to dry myself off."[4]

There was a time when I would have read a list like that and thought, *Man, I can't imagine how rough that would be.* Depression changed all that. No wonder some people call it the "black cloud." All-encompassing darkness is just what it is. And yet slowly but surely my spirits were lifted each time I prayed "with thanksgiving," as Philippians 4:6 says to do.

Therapy: Yep, You Read That Right

Time, touch, and thanksgiving helped me tremendously, and yet the first time I saw the needle not merely move but *jump* was when I let a therapist into my life.

I grew up in an era that had little use for professional therapy, and even into the first few decades of adulthood there was a determined shoving-things-under-the-rug. Especially at church, when someone asked how you were, the correct answer was "Doing great!" The motivation was probably noble; after all, "If Jesus has achieved the victory, why am I so sad?" as author Stephanie Lobdell says.[5]

Following your insistence that you were "doing great," you were then expected to provide substantiation of that condition with two or three irrefutable facts: work was going great, or the kids were doing well in school, or little Johnny hit a home run at his baseball game last weekend. It didn't matter what you said so long as it bore witness to the fact that you were *doing great*. Which is fine when you're actually doing great. But what about the days when you're not?

Remnants of this line of thinking permeated my cancer experience, as I'll detail in chapter 3, and while I'll admit it's more than a little difficult to teach this old dog new tricks, the level of despondency I felt as a result of depression had me urgently dialing for help.

Nearly fifteen years ago, my friend Tommy Nelson, who pastors Denton Bible Church a half an hour's drive northwest of me, stunned his congregation and a wide swath of the Dallas–Fort Worth metroplex that is deeply impacted by his ministry when he admitted that he had been suffering with depression. This great man of God effectively led Prestonwood's Metro Bible study for young adults for many years, so he is a colleague I deeply respect. He is also a tough, straight-shooting former college quarterback who somehow seemed *above* trials like this. And yet one day, as cliché as it sounds, he simply couldn't get himself out of bed.

He described the sensation of depression coming upon him as being hijacked, bushwhacked, blindsided by an unseen force. What had begun as a physical ailment—a racing heartbeat and inexplicable full-body aches and pains for weeks on end—had morphed into an emotional plague that left him feeling hopeless, helpless, and forlorn. If there is one person who was less likely to seek out the services of a professional therapist than I was, Tommy was that man. And yet when his wife, Teresa, told him that he needed to go "talk to someone," despite his weeks-long protest of a plan that included that step, he knew deep down she was right.

One of the elders at Tommy's church had a friend who was a psychiatrist, and upon the elder's explaining Tommy's situation to him, that doctor agreed to see the suffering man. "I should probably mention that he isn't a believer," the elder told Tommy. "In fact, he's a Hindu."

To hear Tommy describe it—which he did in very public ways once he found level footing again—going to this particular therapist made him feel as if he were Saul paying a visit to the witch of Endor.[6] Do you remember this story? Samuel the prophet had died, and Saul had thrown out all the fortune-tellers from the land. But soon enough, feeling threatened now by the Philistine army that had assembled against him and not being able to get God to reply to his urgent pleas for help, Saul summoned his servants and demanded that they point him to a medium. Surely a witch could help. So Saul disguised himself and went to see the woman "by night," says 1 Samuel 28:8, which, incidentally, is the first sign you're probably doing something you ought not to do. Tommy didn't go so far as to disguise himself, but he wondered if the man could help. He changed his tune in short order, though, once the doctor told him exactly what had happened to his body and what he needed to do to heal.

Of course, I knew of this entire turn of events long before I experienced depression myself. And while the version I went through was far different—and far less chronic—than what Tommy had to endure, therapy helped us both. Just as Tommy had done, I humbled myself before a professional counselor, telling him how I was feeling, what I was afraid of, what I needed, and how he could help. He listened. He cared. He prescribed meds when necessary. And he helped get me back on my feet. Whatever you believe about Christians and medication radically changes when you're staring up from the bottom of the black hole known as depression. In Tommy's words, "You get in that state, and . . . you will take rat dung" if it will help get you out.[7]

I couldn't agree more with my friend. Which is why I tell people I meet who are struggling to get themselves to a professional counselor, who can help right whatever is wrong.

Where All Healing Begins

Real gains were made by each of these interventions I mentioned—by giving myself time to recover, by reaching for community and for professional help, by honing the practice of gratitude—but one resource was so valuable to me, so transformative, that it inspired the book you're now holding in your hands. When nothing else worked for me during the yearlong battle with depression, this singular habit rescued me, dragging me time and again from the depths of the pit, setting my feet once again on solid ground so that I could re-engage with life. That habit was returning to, engaging with, prioritizing the Word of God—the truest truth I know.

There were three beautiful by-products of letting God's Word have its way in my mind and heart, the first of which was that the Scriptures reminded me that regardless of how isolated I felt, I was anything but alone. Countless others had walked the path I found myself on, and in the same way God had ministered to them, he was committed to ministering to me. Second, the Scriptures provided me with the power I so desperately sought while stuck in my powerless state. And third, as I prioritized engaging with God's Word even when I didn't feel like doing so, I felt myself coming back to life. My faith was lighting up again because "faith comes from hearing, and hearing through the word of Christ" (Romans 10:17).

I was seen. I could be strong. I would survive another day. When life rips the rug out from underneath you and you're lying there flat on your back, possibilities are tough to come by. I heartily welcomed these.

Never Alone

This wasn't always the case, but during at least a portion of most days, I longed to read my Bible. I'd rise at five in the morning, pour myself a cup of hot coffee, reach for my Bible and journal, and head to my chair. Sometimes I'd play worship music in the background and sometimes I'd opt for silence, but always it was during those unhurried times, just God's Word and me, that I would be strengthened for the days ahead.

I remember finding my way to Numbers 11, where Moses, perhaps the greatest leader in all of antiquity, was left oppressed and overwhelmed by the weighty responsibilities of his role. The people Moses was leading were complaining left and right, and he'd had it. Looking skyward, he said to God, "I cannot carry all these people by myself; the burden is too heavy for me. If this is how you are going to treat me, please go ahead and kill me—if I have found favor in your eyes—and do not let me face my own ruin" (vv. 14–15 NIV).

"Just kill me now!" That was the desire of Moses' heart, and yet thankfully God stayed his hand.

I read of Jonah for the umpteenth time, of how he disobeyed God and wound up in the belly of a fish before surrendering to the purpose God had asked him to pursue. God was offering forgiveness and compassion for the people he had asked Jonah to minister to, and regardless of the punishment Jonah thought those people deserved for disobeying God in the first place, it was *God's* will, not Jonah's, that would prevail. There under a shade tree, which, incidentally, God himself had provided, Jonah realized the futility of his rage. It was God who was in control. It was God who was sovereign. It was God whose ways were unlike any others'. It was God, alone, who was King. "It is better for me to die than to live," Jonah said to his heavenly Father (Jonah 4:8). Again, God stayed his hand.

Or what about David, the man after God's own heart? I reread his story too. He was a hard worker, a wise leader, a powerful warrior, a passionate worshiper, a prolific writer, and, eventually, even a king. And yet underneath his myriad accolades was a man who dealt with debilitating depression from time to time. This is, by the way, why so many of us who have suffered through depression recount pretty much living in the book of Psalms: David, the writer of nearly half of them, completely understands our plight! "How long, O LORD? Will you forget me forever?" begins Psalm 13. "How long will you hide your face from me? How long must I take counsel in my soul and have sorrow in my heart all the day? How long shall my enemy be exalted over me? Consider and answer me, O LORD my God; light up my eyes, lest I sleep the sleep of death, lest my enemy say, 'I have prevailed over him,' lest my foes rejoice because I am shaken" (vv. 1–4).

You can almost see the depression dripping off him, can't you? The despondency. The sorrow. The dim eyes. And yet something in him knew that God hadn't given up on him. Which meant he could make it through one more day. "But I have trusted in your steadfast love," that psalm concludes; "my heart shall rejoice in your salvation" (v. 5).

Even the apostle Paul, known as the greatest Christian ever to live, remarked in one of his letters to the believers at Corinth that he didn't want them to "be unaware . . . of the affliction" Paul and his ministry partners endured while serving in Asia (2 Corinthians 1:8). He then said this: "For we were so utterly burdened beyond our strength that we despaired of life itself" (v. 8).

Paul? The apostle Paul? Despairing of life itself?

Certainly, it's possible that the despair Paul felt was episodic and ephemeral, a whisper of a moment that was gone as quickly as it arrived. Either way, he plumbed the depths in some significant way, which during the depth of my own ordeal was oddly heartening to me.

Of course, the one whose story was most instructive to me was that of the great prophet Elijah, mighty man of God.

Elijah served God during a trying time in the life of the people of Israel, because an evil king, Ahab, was on the throne, and he was married to a wicked queen. There's a reason sane people don't name their newborn baby girls Jezebel; you don't want a Jezebel under your roof.

Rather than crumbling to the immorality and idolatry that ran rampant in the land, Elijah stood firm against it, declaring God's truth in the face of lies. He called for national repentance. He called for widespread revival. And then he did something quite remarkable when he challenged the worshipers of idols to a duel.

Elijah had established quite a reputation for calling a spade a spade with Ahab, which is perhaps why he received this greeting, upon approaching the king one day: "Is it you, you troubler of Israel?" (1 Kings 18:17).

In fact, it was Ahab who had troubled Israel, angering Jehovah God and leading his people astray. And Elijah planned to do something about that injustice. He planned to show his beloved God as strong. "I have not troubled Israel," Elijah said to the king, "but you have, and your father's house, because you have abandoned the commandments of the LORD and followed the Baals. Now therefore send and gather all Israel to me at Mount Carmel, and the 450 prophets of Baal and the 400 prophets of Asherah, who eat at Jezebel's table" (vv. 18–19).

And thus the contest was on.

Two bulls would be given to the men. The animals would be cut into pieces and laid on the wood of a makeshift altar, but no fire would be put to them just yet. Then Ahab would call upon the name of his god—Baal—and Elijah would call upon the name of Jehovah God. Whichever deity rained down fire on the offering would be considered the more powerful god.

Ahab went first. He prayed to Baal. He pleaded with Baal. He screamed at the top of his lungs for Baal to respond to his demands. The text says that the people under Ahab's command even "cut themselves after their custom with swords and lances, until the blood gushed out upon them" (v. 28). And still, "No one answered; no one paid attention" to them (v. 29).

Next was Elijah's turn. Elijah called the people to himself. He repaired the altar, which had been thrown down by Ahab and his cronies. He quietly took twelve stones, representing the twelve sons of Jacob, and built an altar in the name of the Lord. After preparing the altar, he said to God, "O LORD, God of Abraham, Isaac, and Israel, let it be known this day that you are God in Israel, and that I am your servant, and that I have done all these things at your word. Answer me, O LORD, answer me, that this people may know that you, O LORD, are God, and that you have turned their hearts back" (vv. 36–37).

The fire that fell from heaven was great enough to consume not only the entirety of the burnt offering but also the wood, stones, and dirt surrounding it. When the people saw what Jehovah God had done, they "fell on their faces and said, 'The LORD, he is God; the LORD, he is God'" (v. 39). And while this victory for Elijah was decisive, his story most certainly did not end there.

Following a humiliating loss to Elijah, Ahab ran home to Jezebel to tell her everything that had happened. In response, Jezebel sent a messenger to Elijah with a vicious word for him: "May the gods strike me and even kill me if by this time tomorrow I have not killed you just as you killed them" (1 Kings 19:2 NLT). In other words: There is a contract on your life, Elijah. Tomorrow you will be dead.

Now, given Elijah's track record, you might expect him to rise against the wicked Jezebel and show her a thing or two. But our mighty man had had enough. Instead of fighting, he fled. Then, as if taking a page from Jonah's story, he situated himself in the shade of a tree and begged God to take his life.

We never learn of the motivation behind Elijah's request. Initially, the text says that he was running in fear, yet he had faced down fear before. Maybe after all he had been through, this threat of death was just too much. Whatever the cause, the lethal combination of fear and fatigue in this man's life would all but take him down.

What happened next is truly a story for the ages. In response to Elijah's crying out to God, God not only came near to the weary one and spoke to him but he also let his divine presence be seen. In 1 Kings 19:11, God said to his weary warrior, "Go out and stand before me on the mountain" (NLT). And as Elijah stood there, God passed by, not as a terrifying earthquake, not as a consuming fire, but as a gentle whisper. Just what Elijah needed.

I have to tell you, as I reread that passage I'd come across scores of times before, I felt for a moment like the black cloud had parted, letting fragments of sunlight in. This is the magnificent message of these timeless stories of Scripture, the assurance that we're never alone. Frankly, I'm relieved that God included real-life stories of people's battles with anxious thoughts. I don't like talking about my own battle with anxiety, but if he can use others' stories of victory over anxiety and depression in my life, then maybe he can use my story in yours.

Plugging Back In

There was a second reason I relished the Scriptures with newfound appreciation during my trial by fire, which is that it provided a much-needed energy source.

If depression takes one thing from you, it's your power. Your energy. Your zest for life. It's not just that you cease experiencing positive emotions such as delight, satisfaction, and joy; it's that you cease feeling *any* emotion—good or bad. You're bottomed out. You're empty. You're flatlined. You're blank. You're existing in quicksand where "the harder you struggle, the deeper you sink."[8] You're unplugged from the you-ness of you.

What God was eager to show me was that *he* was still plugged into life and that his Word was my extension cord. After the apostle

Paul pleaded with the Lord three times to remove the thorn in the flesh he was dealing with, God said to him, "My grace is sufficient for you, for my power is made perfect in weakness" (2 Corinthians 12:9). "Therefore," Paul said, "I will boast all the more gladly of my weaknesses, so that the power of Christ may rest upon me. For the sake of Christ, then, I am content with weaknesses, insults, hardships, persecutions, and calamities. For when I am weak, then I am strong" (vv. 9–10).

If Paul's situation could be extrapolated to my own, then God must have experienced a *serious* surge of strength each time he looked upon the hamstrung life of Jack Graham. Now, if only he'd pass some to me.

As I came to the Scriptures each day—some days grudgingly—I began to sense an uplift in my spirit. The passage that came to mind nearly every time I cracked open my Bible is from Hebrews 4. "For the word of God is living and active," it reads, "sharper than any two-edged sword, piercing to the division of soul and of spirit, of joints and of marrow, and discerning the thoughts and intentions of the heart. And no creature is hidden from his sight, but all are naked and exposed to the eyes of him to whom we must give account" (vv. 12–13).

Those words were a promise to me, a gift. They represented motion when life felt still, energy when life felt flat, decisiveness when life felt vague, recognition when life felt bleak. *I see you,* God's Word seemed to be whispering to me. *I can help you. My precepts will help bring you back to life....*

The same God who spoke the world into existence quite literally spoke his Word into being. Yes, more than forty human authors on three different continents were tapped across 1,500 years to pen in three different languages the sentences and paragraphs that make up its sixty-six books, but it was God himself who was speaking, God who was literally *inspiring*—breathing—the Word. Further, this Word of God is active, which means it still speaks to us today. Bible translator J. B. Phillips is said to have remarked that during a season when he was working on a translation of the New Testament, he felt as if he were "rewiring an old house with the electricity still on."[9]

The Bible is alive. It's dynamic. It's filled with explosive *power*. The power to convert; the power to cleanse; the power to correct; the power to comfort. Whatever power you're in need of, the Bible is your ultimate source.

And the Bible is *accurate*, Hebrews 4 tells us, penetrating the deepest recesses of our hearts and souls. The writer of Hebrews describes it as "sharper than any two-edged sword," which speaks not of a long bayonet, but rather of a slight, double-bladed, eighteen-inch *makhaira*—a weapon of proximity, a weapon of precision, a weapon to be prized.

Even in my lackluster state, I could feel the power. The strength. The miraculous impact in my life. Waves of fresh awareness would often wash over me regarding the Bible's importance to those of us trying to sort out life on planet Earth. Truly, what other book can boast of the Bible's historical prominence in the world? "The grass withers, the flower fades," Isaiah 40:8 says, "but the word of our God will stand forever."

And indeed it has. What other book has been burned and banned and outlawed as often as the Bible? What other book has withstood such vicious attacks?

What other book has been translated into more than 600 languages? (Did you know that 600 languages even existed?) Include dialects of those languages and the figure skyrockets to 2,500.

What other book has had such widespread appeal? (Current statistics point to lifetime Bible sales of more than five billion copies. Even J. K. Rowling can't compete with that.)

What other book has influenced history, the nations' governments, the curricula of universities, and classical literature more than the Bible has?

What other book has been the source of *other* books as much as the Bible has?

No other book boasts this list of accolades. The Word of God, with its history and its prophecy, its poetry and its drama, its stories of love and its stories of war,[10] its unmatched delivery of truth—this book stands alone.

Coming Back to Life

The third benefit I realized as I let God's Word guide my thoughts, my attitudes, my actions, and my desires was that despite my fear that I'd feel emotionally dead forever, I started coming back to life. In 2 Timothy 3, the apostle Paul calls this process "continu[ing] in what you have learned and have firmly believed" (v. 14). "But as for you," the full passage reads, "continue in what you have learned and have firmly believed, knowing from whom you learned it and how from childhood you have been acquainted with the sacred writings, which are able to make you wise for salvation through faith in Christ Jesus" (vv. 14–15).

Paul then helps us to understand what it looks like to "continue in" what we have learned and believed by describing the effects we ought to see unfold in our lives as we allow Scripture to guide our lives. Verses 16 and 17 read: "All Scripture is breathed out by God and profitable for teaching, for reproof, for correction, and for training in righteousness, that the man of God may be complete, equipped for every good work."

I have loved the Bible since I was a child. I loved reading it. I loved memorizing it. I loved thinking about what I'd learned. But according to this passage in 2 Timothy, that love for the Bible was only the first step in a four-step progression. Yes, it was wonderful that I enjoyed the *intake* of Scripture, but was I similarly prioritizing its outtake?

Staying with verse 17 above, we realize that God intends for his Word not only to teach us what is his will and what are his ways but also to equip us for taking that education to a world in need of his forgiveness, his compassion, his grace. This is accomplished, according to that same passage, by God showing us where we have gone astray—that's the "reproof" part; by God helping us correct our ways and bring our will into alignment with his once more; and by God inviting us to work with him to restore this world according to his original intent. To truly "love God's Word," then, means loving not just the part where we learn what it says but also loving the transformation it effects in our lives.

"Let the word of Christ dwell in you richly, teaching and admonishing one another in all wisdom," wrote the apostle Paul in Colossians 3:16, "singing psalms and hymns and spiritual songs, with thankfulness in your hearts to God." As it turns out, the more I exposed myself to the truth of God's Word, even if deep under the surface of what anxiety and depression would allow me to discern, the more this promising progression you and I looked at had its desired effect.

Life Comes for Us All

Dr. Tim Clinton has reported that up to 20 percent of the population will at some point in their lives "suffer from major depressive and dysthymic disorders."[11] (Incidentally, he also acknowledges that women are twice as likely as men to deal with depression, which is why until my diagnosis I never gave the disease a second thought.) This figure means that one out of every five people walking the planet will at some point be walking under that black cloud. I don't know if you have been one of those five, or if you are one of those five right now, but I do know that eventually life comes for us all. Perhaps (and hopefully!) not with the force of a knockout punch, but in some form or fashion we all will struggle from time to time.

News reports of suffering halfway around the globe weigh on our hearts.

A child rebels.

A marriage falls apart.

A beloved spouse dies.

You lose your job.

Your health feels frail.

Chronic pain won't let up, no matter how many specialists you see.

"In the last days there will come times of difficulty," Paul wrote to his protégé, Timothy—and, by extension, to us (2 Timothy 3:1). *Difficult* doesn't even begin to describe our experience down here, wouldn't you agree? "Pain is the hallmark of mortality," wrote coauthors Dr. Paul Brand and Philip Yancey in their marvelous book *Fearfully and Wonderfully*.[12]

We are not merely spiritual beings; we are spiritual beings having a physical existence, and that added phrase makes all the difference in the world. These bodies of ours—our brains, our backs, our blood, our skin—so much of how we fare in this regard is simply out of our control. Ditto for our emotions. And yet sadly—in the context of the local church, anyway—we have been trained from the youngest of ages to shade the truth when asked how these selves of ours are doing. As author Marc Brackett says in his book *Permission to Feel*, "There are hundreds of words we could use to describe our feelings, but most of us use one or two: 'fine' or 'busy.'"[13]

This phenomenon showed up in my refusal to let my church know of my prostate surgery until after it was clear to me that my recovery was going to take longer than I expected. In true therapy-averse fashion, I distinctly remember telling plenty of people during that twentieth-anniversary celebration at Prestonwood that I was "doing great!" despite my barely being able to walk. The first time I preached on depression—and fessed up regarding my personal struggles—people approached me in droves to tell me of the similar battles they'd faced. How long had they felt locked up by the church's unwillingness to address the issues pervading our congregation—not to mention our world at large? Now that I knew better, I vowed to do better. I vowed to welcome them from their hiding spots. I vowed to come out from my own.

As it relates to you, please carefully read what I'm about to write: If you are struggling—with depression or with any other debilitating challenge—know that you're not alone. I get it. I care about your story. You are known. You are loved. You can be healed. You don't have to be afraid of the cloud, as menacing as it looks. You don't have to stay bound up in darkness. You don't have to hide your struggle, your pain.

You can find your way out of the pit you've landed in. God's Word will be your rope.

———

During the twelve months it took for me to make my climb toward daylight again, by his grace God brought to mind a steady stream of Bible passages, many of which I'd written on my heart as a boy. Those passages will show up as the epigraphs to each chapter in this book, such as the passage from 2 Timothy 3 that kicked off this chapter. In the same way that these anointed words encouraged me, I hope they will encourage you, regardless of where you are on your journey of faith. You may be a new believer who is trying to sort out this thing called Christianity. In that case, the balance of this book will feel like something of a spiritual primer that explains the foundations of our faith, explores the primary pitfalls believers often find themselves in, and expresses the central tasks we are to be about as we walk through our earthly life.

You may be spiritually unconvinced, someone who isn't altogether sure how you wound up reading a book by a late-aged Baptist preacher from the South. If that is you, *welcome*. I pray you experience a deep-seated peace as you take in the concepts to come.

But it's also true that you may be a veteran believer, someone who has long walked with Jesus, someone who has "been there and done that" and taken home the T-shirt as proof. I'll show my cards early here: *You are the one I'm writing to*. This is why I titled the book *Reignite* instead of *Ignite*. It is my firm belief that I am far from the only person out there who required a life-leveling experience to reignite my faith in what I say I believe. I love the Lord, I love the Scriptures, I love walking with God. And yet even I concede that it is far too easy to get a little sloppy in our spiritual lives. It's far too easy to coast on yesterday's convictions instead of seeking out truth for today.

And so, this book. I've included the Scripture passages to minister to your possibly weak and world-weary soul, but I also hope you will be reunited with the God of your salvation, allowing him to lead you to a few "anchor texts" of your own. If you're game, then you can begin the practice of prioritizing God's Word even now. Let's look at the four aspects that served me well and see if they resonate with you.

The Only Reliable Rescue Rope

I was on my phone the other day when a little notification popped up, telling me that my weekly report was ready for viewing. I clicked on it, and that is when I learned that my screen time was a full 7 percent lower that week than it had been the week before. I'm not going to tell you what either week's total was, because I have no interest in indicting myself. What I will say is this: When you or I complain about not having fifteen minutes a day to sit down in a quiet spot, crack open our Bibles, and read the blessed Word, we are telling a bald-faced lie. Read your Bible, my friend. I challenge you to shut off your screen and open God's Word. That is step number one.

Read God's Word

It's easy to read the Bible every day. Think of it: You either own a copy of the Book or else you can access it for free online. A full hundred-plus versions of the Bible are now in print, which means we can read God's Word in a style that is effortless to consume. And we no longer live in an age when we have to spend 80 percent of our waking lives tilling soil, growing food, harvesting food, or cooking food. A tap on the DoorDash app and we're done. We have access. And we have time. What more do we need?

The irony, of course, is that what makes it easy to read the Bible every day is also what makes it hard. Anything in abundance loses its value, and other stuff is constantly competing for our time. And so we miss a day and think, *Eh, I'll do it tomorrow.* Then tomorrow comes, and we miss that day too. Soon an entire week has flown by, then a year, two years, without the Good Book getting read.

My advice to you and me both is this: Systematize your reading so that it's part of your usual flow. Find a spot, declare a time, and open the Bible—it doesn't have to be more complicated than that. If you don't know where to begin, may I suggest the book of John, the fourth book in the New Testament, just after Matthew, Mark, and Luke? You may want to grab a journal and a pen so you can write down what you're thinking as you read. I know this sounds elementary, but the best practices often are. Like me, you probably can look back on your life and see seasons when God's Word just oozed from your pores. You read the Scriptures with such devotion that they quite literally shaped your thoughts. I'm inviting you to return to that love, to return to the priority you once held.

To go one step further, heed the advice of the brilliant Bible teacher Kay Arthur, who popularized the "inductive" approach to Scripture reading. For starters, she says to read and then reread the passage or book you're focusing on. Next, identify the type of literature with which you are dealing. Is it poetry? Allegory? A letter to a specific people group? Third, answer objective questions of the text—the who, what, when, where, why, and how involved. Fourth, identify the facts about any people and events mentioned. Fifth, read and reread the text until you discover the words and phrases that are repeated, then mark those in distinctive ways. And finally, identify the main theme at hand.[14]

This type of approach obviously necessitates more than a quick flyby for the purpose of checking "Bible reading" off your list. But anything worth doing is worth doing well, yes? "A book that requires nothing from you might offer the same diversion as that of a television sitcom, but it is unlikely to provide intellectual, aesthetic, or spiritual rewards long after the cover is closed,"[15] writes Karen Swallow Prior. Every minute I have dedicated to reading God's Word has been returned to me in quality of life a hundredfold.

Meditate on God's Word

Read God's Word, then *meditate* on what you've read. Through the years, I've made it my practice to meditate on the Scriptures for the purpose of memorizing them, because once they are written on your mind, on your heart, you can call them up at a moment's notice, no flipping of pages or swiping of screens required. You may recall that when Jesus was made to square off against Satan in the desert, each time Satan offered a temptation, Jesus responded with truth from God's Word. He didn't have to say, "Hang on a sec. I know there's a verse about this somewhere. . . ." No, he had God's truth at the ready, right there when he needed it. I'm always amused by people who claim to treasure the "sword of the Spirit," as the Bible is called in Ephesians 6, but who then leave that sword in the sheath nearly every moment of every day. Success happens when preparation meets opportunity. And so, sit with God's Word.

Ponder God's Word.

Meditate on God's Word, not just "*reading* Scripture or *studying* Scripture or even thinking *about* Scripture," writes Robert Morgan, but rather "*thinking* Scripture."[16]

Yes! Turn God's Word over in your mind time and again, until his precepts are knitted to you. For my part, I'd camp out in the Psalms day after day, reading and rereading, chewing and mulling, considering and applying, poking at each concept from every side. "Intermeddle with all knowledge," the great British preacher Charles Spurgeon once said in a lecture to his seminary students, "but above all things meditate day and night in the law of the Lord."[17] May we be like John Bunyan, writer of *The Pilgrim's Progress*, about whom Spurgeon wrote, "Prick him anywhere—his blood is Bibline, the very essence of the Bible flows from him."

Nothing will energize you like the Word of God flowing through your life.

Pray Over God's Word

We're about to spend the entirety of chapter 2 on the profitability of prayer, so I will be brief here and simply acknowledge that after you read and meditate on God's Word, the most beneficial next step you can choose to take is to speak his Word right back to him in prayer. I often turn my daily walk into a prayer walk, using the Scriptures I just encountered to fuel dialogue with God.

Just as you'd likely take immense delight in hearing one of your children read aloud a heartfelt letter you'd written to him or her, I imagine God leans forward and tunes in each time you or I recount for him the parts of his Word that are proving most meaningful to us.

Proclaim God's Word

Finally, *proclaim* the Word of God. The most agonizing aspect of the early days of my bout with depression was being sidelined from preaching the Scriptures to the congregation I adore. But guess what I learned during that season? I don't have to be standing on a stage in a massive auditorium to accomplish the proclamation of God's holy Word. As I began to emerge from the cocoon of despair I'd been in, I found that verses from the Bible were flowing naturally again from my lips. Sometimes I was the only person listening! And yet even then I was being ministered to.

God's Word is too good to keep to ourselves, which is why this fourth step is so vital. As we point people to truth—whether ourselves or others we meet—we stimulate spiritual growth. "Revive me, O LORD, according to Your word," the psalmist wrote in Psalm 119:107 (NKJV), which reminds us that revival indeed comes by way of God's Word. Souls are heartened and lives saved when we impart even a glimmer of the gospel to a pair of listening ears. "So faith comes from hearing," Romans 10:17 testifies, "and hearing through the Word of Christ."

I will tell you that I have seen addicts break their addiction, all from absorbing the Word of the Lord.

I have seen prisoners accept forgiveness and experience a sort of internal freedom, all from absorbing the Word of the Lord.

I have seen broken marriages restored—I'm talking divorced couples choosing to *come back together again*—all from absorbing the Word of the Lord.

I have seen the physically infirm take back healthfulness, all from absorbing the Word of the Lord.

I have seen a man suffering from severe insomnia, listlessness, hopelessness, depression—there in the mirror, I saw him—and find his stride again, all from absorbing the Word of the Lord.

When we speak out the truth that we have internalized, lives can't help but be changed. I ask you to test me in this and see if it isn't true: As you prioritize engagement with the Scriptures—reading them, meditating on them and memorizing them, praying them back to God, proclaiming them multiple times each day—what you will begin to enjoy is a certain *completeness* in life, which is God's Word having its way in you.

2

Prayer That Never Fails

Prayer is the natural outgushing of a soul in communion with Jesus.

Charles Spurgeon, "The Secret of Power in Prayer"

The Lord is the everlasting God, the Creator of the ends of the earth. He does not faint or grow weary; his understanding is unsearchable. He gives power to the faint, and to him who has no might he increases strength. Even youths shall faint and be weary, and young men shall fall exhausted; but they who wait for the Lord shall renew their strength; they shall mount up with wings like eagles; they shall run and not be weary; they shall walk and not faint.

Isaiah 40:28–31

While the specific scene is well-known, the surrounding context is not. First, the scene: In Matthew 14, we find Jesus withdrawing to a boat in search of some alone time. But this wasn't to be, for as the New Testament Scriptures substantiate, when a crowd learned that Jesus was nearby, the crowd always crowded him.

"Now when Jesus heard this [news of John the Baptist's death]," the text says, "he withdrew from there in a boat to a desolate place by himself. But when the crowds heard it, they followed him on foot from the towns. Now when it was evening, the disciples came to him and said, 'This is a desolate place, and the day is now over; send the crowds away to go into the villages and buy food for themselves.' But Jesus said, 'They need not go away; you give them something to eat.' They said to him, 'We have only five loaves here and two fish'" (vv. 13, 15–17).

If you have been a believer for any length of time, then you know how this story ends. Jesus took the paltry offering from his disciples, who had those morsels only because a little boy had donated his sack lunch, and he fed every person gathered there. But while this story of "the feeding of the five thousand" is familiar to most of us, what's rarely talked about is the fact that as Jesus came to this set of circumstances that day, he was in a heavily burdened state. There was a reason he was headed out to be alone: His friend John the Baptist had just been killed.

By way of context, the ruler of the land, King Herod the tetrarch, was celebrating his birthday when in his revelry he promised his daughter, Salome, the granting of one wish. Her wish—prompted by her mother, who hated anything that threatened the king's vast power—was for John the Baptist's head to be delivered to her on a platter. We don't know if it was that John's power had wooed people away from Herod's influence or if it was that John was a bold truth teller and that did him in, but whatever the reason, Herod wanted John dead.

Sort of.

More the case, he wanted to please his wife and daughter, and that meant killing John, despite his feeling "sorry" for the act, as Matthew 14:9 details. (If you're truly sorry for the fact that you're about to behead someone, shouldn't that person keep his head?)

The disciples had run to tell Jesus of what had happened to John, and it was upon Jesus' absorbing this sobering report that he had sought solitude, silence, peace.

But then: crowds.

Always the crowds.

Life was coming at Jesus with full force, and he couldn't get away. Jesus was pressured and pushed. Yes, he was 100 percent God. But he was also 100 percent man. And our Savior needed some rest.

Sound familiar? Circumstances hit you. Things feel heavy. Life seems out of control. And yet you're expected to show up, to care, to serve. This is stress in all her glory—and also just plain life on planet Earth.

Stress All Around

Most likely, you can relate to how Jesus was feeling that day.. For most of us, the nagging, sometimes debilitating sensation of being pulled in too many directions, of perceiving "that demands [on one's life] exceed the personal and social resources the individual is able to mobilize,"[1] as the American Institute of Stress (AIS) reports some dictionaries as defining stress, has become such a pervasive part of life that we hardly remember there is any other way to live.

When thinking about stress, I always come back to five Cs. *Change* can cause stress, whether it is a change of job, a change of residence, a change in relationships, a change in health. *Conflict* can cause stress—relational conflict, political conflict, even a sense of emotional confliction within yourself. *Criticism* can cause stress: Your boss is unhappy with your work, your spouse is dissatisfied in your marriage, your friend is disappointed about your distance, and these people all decide to let you know. *Concerns of the day* can cause stress, including everything from the state of affairs in our nation to the fact that your car's tires are balding and you don't have time to get to the shop. We can also face *crises* in life, which of course cause great stress. A loved one receives a terrible medical diagnosis. A sudden job loss upsets your financial footing. A scandal rocks your church community. A child makes a decision you know he will someday regret.

Incidentally, my son Jason, who is a dad himself, told me I should include a sixth C: *children*. As he put it, "Kids cause more stress than the other five categories combined."

He may have a point.

Whatever the cause, stress tends to show up in our lives not just from time to time, but rather *most* of the time, seemingly with the goal of reminding us that we are in the rat race, and the rats are winning. And each time it shows up, a predictable pattern unfolds: We encounter the stressor, and we gear up for action; our heart rate increases, maybe even skipping a beat; our blood pressure rises as adrenaline kicks into overdrive; our hands begin to sweat and shake a little; our muscles tighten; our senses heighten; cortisol floods our bloodstream as we weigh our options. Do we run from the stress to avoid it, or do we run toward it to conquer it? Will we flee or will we fight?

I always picked the fight.

For years—decades even—I thought that this progression was pretty fun. I'm a type A guy for whom stress was a welcome addition to my life. Stress meant *excitement*. Stress meant *challenge*. Stress meant *movement*. Stress meant *go time*. I had heard about "eustress," the positive kind of stress that fires you up and compels you to take action, providing a pleasurable dopamine hit once you do. As far as I could tell, stress was not a foe but a friend. "I don't get stressed," I would jokingly proclaim. "I *give* stress."

My team and I would have a good laugh about this—that is, until it wasn't funny anymore.

The reason the laughter died down is because the stress I'd once regarded as a motivator became an outright monster in my life. My mind was no longer able to deal with the pressure. My body began malfunctioning on me. Over time, my sense of optimism dulled. The dam that held my life and leadership intact had finally given way, and a terrifying flood ensued. Overwhelmed is no way to live.

According to the AIS, 55 percent of people in the United States experience "stress during the day," and a full 83 percent of the nation's workers deal with work-related stress, which "causes 120,000 deaths and results in $190 billion in healthcare costs" each year.[2]

No laughing matter, to be sure.

In a 2017 survey conducted by the American Psychological Association and reported by the AIS, the top stressors of those polled included our nation's future, money, work, the political climate, and violence or crime. Three years prior, in a similar survey, 77 percent of people surveyed said that the stress they experienced day by day caused them to regularly experience negative physical symptoms—fatigue, headaches, muscle tension, gastrointestinal discomfort, dizziness, teeth grinding, a change in sex drive, and more. Half said stress was having a negative effect on their personal and professional lives. Almost half said their stress level had worsened over the past five years. A third of those experiencing psychological symptoms said they felt on the verge of needing to cry.[3]

I have also seen stats reporting that up to 90 percent of the people who visit their primary-care physicians are there because of a stress-related cause.[4] The question isn't so much whether or not we will encounter stress in life, but rather how we will respond once we do.

Lashing Out or Looking Up

Back to our scene involving Jesus and the crowds of hungry people. They were hungry for food, yes, but also hungry for attention, for healing, for help. And this was far from an isolated episode for the Messiah; try to name a time in Scripture when Jesus wasn't surrounded by demanding people, and you'll come up woefully short. As is the case for you and me today, so many needs came knocking for Jesus that we wouldn't have faulted him for eventually refusing to come to the door. That's what we'd probably do, anyway! For our part, in the face of a stress overload, we'd rather stick our heads in the sand. Or escape through food or drink. Or scroll ourselves silly on social media. Or bury ourselves in work. We'd rather shout to anyone listening that this insanity simply must stop! But when those stressors showed up at Jesus' feet, compounding the personal burden he already bore, he responded in the most curious of ways. Instead of lashing out, Jesus decided to look up.

Here's the fuller story from Matthew 14:

> When he [Jesus] went ashore he saw a great crowd, and he had compassion on them and healed their sick. Now when it was evening, the disciples came to him and said, "This is a desolate place, and the day is now over; send the crowds away to go into the villages and buy food for themselves." But Jesus said, "They need not go away; you give them something to eat." They said to him, "We have only five loaves here and two fish." And he said, "Bring them here to me." Then he ordered the crowds to sit down on the grass, and taking the five loaves and the two fish, he looked up to heaven and said a blessing. Then he broke the loaves and gave them to the disciples, and the disciples gave them to the crowds. And they all ate and were satisfied. And they took up twelve baskets full of the broken pieces left over. And those who ate were about five thousand men, besides women and children.
>
> vv. 14–21

With the situational stress level sky-high, instead of pushing the sources of that stress away, Jesus invited them to come closer still. He looked toward heaven and prayed to his Father. He paused to give thanks for his Father's provision. And then he cooperated with God's grand plan—in this case, miraculously turning a small snack into an all-you-can-eat buffet. It seems so simple that if we're not careful, we might just miss it: look up . . . trust . . . serve.

Yes, lashing out was certainly an option, but far wiser, Jesus knew, was *looking up*. "Prayer is the slender nerve," Charles Spurgeon once said, "that moves the muscles of Omnipotence."[5] When stress is mounting and power is failing, prayer is the surest way through. Which is why we see Jesus during his earthly ministry so often pulling away to pray, prioritizing the practice of prayer. "But he [Jesus] would withdraw to desolate places and pray," Luke 5:16 says. "And after he had taken leave of them," Mark 6:46 says, "he went up on the mountain to pray." "In these days he went out to the mountain to pray," Luke 6:12 confirms, "and all night he continued in prayer to God." Mark 1:35 says, "And rising very early in the morning, while it was still dark, he departed and went out to a desolate place, and there he prayed."

Luke 11:1: "Jesus was praying in a certain place, and when he finished, one of his disciples said to him, 'Lord, teach us to pray, as John taught his disciples.'"

Matthew 19:13: "Then children were brought to him that he might lay his hands on them and pray."

Matthew 26:36: "Then Jesus went with them to a place called Gethsemane, and he said to his disciples, 'Sit here, while I go over there and pray.'"

You get the feeling from watching this pattern of prayer in Jesus' life that he was interested in far more than *talking a good game* where obedience to his Father was concerned. You realize he *was actually connecting* with God. And so, time and time again, Jesus would talk to the Father. He would rest in the Father. And there he'd be equipped to help further the Father's plan. "For thus said the Lord GOD, the Holy One of Israel," we read in Isaiah 30:15, "'In returning and rest you shall be saved; in quietness and in trust shall be your strength.'"

Which is precisely what Jesus chose to do.

He returned to his Father.

He rested in God's care.

He strengthened himself by praying.

Returning to God

As Jesus' life bore out, you and I could pursue righteousness every moment of every day and yet *still*, owing to the brokenness of this world, encounter debilitating stress. More often, however, we bring stressful situations onto ourselves. Take the nation of Israel, for example. The catalyst for the prophet Isaiah's compelling God's chosen people to "return and rest" was that they had been doing the very opposite of those things: running frantically from God and his will. "'Ah, stubborn children,' declares the LORD, 'who carry out a plan, but not mine,'" Isaiah 30:1–2 says, "'and who make an alliance, but not of my Spirit, that they may add sin to sin; who set out to go down to Egypt, without asking for my direction, to take refuge in the protection of Pharaoh and to seek shelter in the shadow of Egypt!'"

Here, the prophet was reprimanding us. We know what it is to be stubborn, to carry out plans that are not of God, and to take refuge in people and priorities that aren't his best for us. And to seek shelter from someone besides him. "Return," the prophet says, essentially. "Turn around. Head for home. Go back."

I've found that advice to be sound.

When you and I encounter stress of any kind—whether because we are running too fast and too hard, or whether we're just in the wrong place at the wrong time when life decides to kick up some dust—we can learn to let our reflexive reaction be what Jesus' was: to refuse to run, or to rant, or to rage, and instead choose to *return to God*.

Resting in God

And then there is this: Once we return to God, we are handed the luxury of resting in him. Oh, what an exhale you ought to experience the moment you rest in his care. "Return to me," God beckons us, "so that I can care for you." And with that, every believer's shoulders should fall as every last burden is finally relieved.

Is now the right time to admit that I stink at this? I am the worst when it comes to rest. And yet when you have aged as much as I have, you "sage" a little too—or at least that's how it's supposed to work. One bit of wisdom I have picked up along the way—100 percent through trial and error—is that I make for a terrible god. How desperately I need God's unparalleled care to face this thing called life. And based on the countless conversations I have with all sorts of people each week, I'm guessing that you do too.

If I had to put a number to it, I'd say that for every ten people I talk to, at least six of them are worn out. They won't let on that this is the case right away, but if we have ten or more minutes to talk with each other, the truth comes spilling out. "I'm exhausted," they'll admit. "I'm wrung out. I'm tired at a level that makes me worried I'll never, ever catch up."

They don't know how they got to where they are, and they don't know how to get out of it; all they know is that their system is close to utterly and completely shutting down. They've been eating the "bread of anxious toil," as Psalm 127:2 calls it, and those slices are rancid, stiff, and stale.

I was told of a group of Americans who had gone on a safari in the African bush, and every morning they were up with the sun, pushing their tour guides to go, go, go. There were animals to see, new places to explore, adventures to be had. Eventually, after a string of eleven sunup-to-sundown days, the guides pushed back. "No," they told their full-throttle clients, "we must let our souls catch up with our bodies. Today, our friends, we rest."

That sort of soul catch-up is exactly what so many of us need. We return to God and choose to rest in him because the detoxification we're searching for requires a purification that's *divine*.

There are two points I want to draw your attention to on this issue of resting in God. First, God is eager for us to come to him. I don't know what kind of image you hold of God the Father in your mind and heart, but he welcomes you into his presence. The story is told of a man in the eighteenth century who fell off his horse while crossing a rushing river and feared he would drown. Along came a group of men, including Thomas Jefferson, the great statesman and third president of the United States. After the fallen man noticed the group, he looked directly at Mr. Jefferson and, despite his having no idea who it was he was looking at, cried out to him, specifically, for help. He was asked later why he chose Jefferson to be his rescuer, to which he answered, "Because he had a *yes* face."

Our heavenly Father has a yes face. He loves when we return to him, and he loves when we trust him to provide for our needs. Think of it this way: If my grandson Ian were climbing a tree and got himself stuck on a high branch, and I happened to walk by, do you think that if I heard Ian crying out for help, I'd walk on by? Do you think I'd say, "Well, Ian, Daddy Jack can't help you until I know how your grades were last semester." Do you think I'd waste even one second getting to him, catching him, cradling him, making sure he was all right?

Our Father feels the same way about us. Every time Deb and I visit the Middle East, we hear Jewish boys and girls trailing their earthly fathers, saying, "Abba! Abba!" *Daddy! Daddy!* God is our Abba—our Daddy. Our heavenly Father who cares. We can come "*boldly* to the throne of grace," Hebrews 4:16 says, "that we may obtain mercy and find grace to help in time of need" (NKJV, emphasis added). Hallelujah for God's willingness to welcome us lovingly whenever we're weary. "Come," he says with a smile on his face. "Come. Sit down. *Just rest.*"

But that's not all, for there is a second dynamic at work: God is not only willing to replenish us whenever we need to be restored but he is also *able* to do this good work. His rest is active, you might say, refusing to leave us in a depleted state. Our bodies are his temple, 1 Corinthians 6:19–20 tells us, which means that God cares deeply about us—body, soul, and mind. If we wear out these bodies, then where will we live? God is committed to keeping us vibrant and healthy, energized and equipped, active and enthusiastic, strong and sound. The only question is whether we'll accept his bold offer of compassion, generosity, and grace.

Letting Salvation Run Its Course

The result of returning to God and resting in God's sufficiency, of course, is deliverance. We are delivered from our stubbornness. We are delivered from our willfulness. We are delivered from our worldly priorities. We are delivered from our stress. We are delivered, in effect, from *ourselves*.

Recently I asked a friend of mine at Prestonwood named Tait to share his story of returning to and resting in God with our entire congregation, and with courage to spare he said yes. To hear Tait tell it, for nearly two decades he and his wife had prioritized the "North Dallas lifestyle," which, if we're painting with a broad brush, includes buying as much house as the mortgage lender will allow you, upgrading your vehicles to luxury class, signing up for exclusive country clubs and health clubs, and putting your children in nationally recognized private schools. After Tait and his wife had checked all these boxes, they were "hit with a terminally ill child," he said. "We spent the next two hundred fifty nights in a hospital, our stress levels now through the roof."

Soon enough, the stress of their child's ailing health began to affect Tait's wife as well. Her health was plummeting as they were forced to say goodbye to their young child.

"I felt aimless," Tait said. "I was grieving. I should have been in counseling, but I thought I could handle things. It felt like I was driving my old college beater with a giant eighteen-wheeler on my tail. Eventually, I couldn't outrun the load. I had to acknowledge my pain."

Before the couple had fully worked through the loss of their young son, they decided to adopt two children—a brother and a sister—who had been abused. "Our stress skyrocketed again," Tait said.

Tait explained that, for several years, he and his wife operated on "a razor's edge," with emotional outbursts erupting like geysers when they least expected them. Worried that they were irreparably damaging their relationship, they finally cried out for help. Nothing magical happened. But as they were faithful to return to God, to rest in God, trusting him to meet their deep-seated needs, the ship of their lives that had been capsized began slowly to be righted again.

If you have ever had an end-of-your-rope experience on par with Tait's, then you know that what I'm about to say is true: The reason we can count trials as joy, as James exhorts us to do in James 1:2–8, is because we understand that facing trials—troubles, struggles, obstacles, stresses, difficulties, problems, pain—is a pathway to returning to and resting in God. Trials are the most effective catalyst for prayer, and when we encounter them, we're quick to run home.

As we are faithful to look to our Father for the comfort and confidence that he alone can provide, we untangle ourselves from the knots that stress ties in our lives. We are now freed up to journey with him. "Come to me, all who labor and are heavy laden," the Lord says to us in Matthew 11:28–30, "and I will give you rest. Take my yoke upon you, and learn from me, for I am gentle and lowly in heart, and you will find rest for your souls. For my yoke is easy, and my burden is light."

We can be afflicted but not crushed, the apostle Paul reminds us in 2 Corinthians 4:8–9.

We can be perplexed but not driven to despair.

We can be persecuted but not forsaken.

We can be struck down but not destroyed.

We can absorb all kinds of stressful situations in this life and still not lose our way when we are careful to respond as Jesus himself responded: returning, resting, being freed up to cooperate with God . . . not lashing out at the challenges of life, but rather stepping back and looking up.

What to Say When You Pray

Most believers I come across want to know one thing about prayer: *What on earth do I say?* And while we will now spend some time addressing that question overtly, the reason why you are this far into a chapter on prayer without my once having mentioned what to say when you pray is because if you get the *context* of prayer right, the *content* matters not. Bold statement, right? Let me back it up.

In Romans 8, perhaps the most profound chapter in all the Bible, the apostle Paul assures us that "the Spirit helps us in our weakness" (v. 26). "For we do not know what to pray for as we ought," he continues, "but the Spirit himself intercedes for us with groanings too deep for words. And he who searches hearts knows what is the mind of the Spirit, because the Spirit intercedes for the saints according to the will of God. And we know that for those who love God all things work together for good, for those who are called according to his purpose" (vv. 26–28).

The weight of Paul's words is in their presumption: Paul *doesn't* say, "If you are one of the substandard believers who can't figure out what to say to God when you pray, then we have a remedial class you can be part of where you can receive some extra help." No, what he does instead is to assume that we as believers will be tongue-tied most of the time. We *all* are weak when it comes to prayer. *Nobody* knows what to say. We *all* need help from the Spirit if we ever hope to "pray as we ought."

I'll also mention here the words of Proverbs 16:1–2, which say, "The plans of the heart belong to man, but the answer of the tongue is from the Lord. All the ways of a man are pure in his own eyes, but the Lord weighs the spirit."

If you can come away from those two passages—not to mention the entirety of Scripture, for that matter—and not see the through line of God's warm, nonjudgmental acceptance of his children into his presence, then you may need to read them again. My point is this: If throughout the course of your days, regardless of whether you've encountered success or stress or both within ten minutes' time, your inclination is to return to your heavenly Father to commune with him and to slow your pace to enjoy his rest, then his Spirit—the Holy Spirit—will *gladly* take things from there.

Our role is the returning, the resting; his is the discerning of hearts.

Now, at the same time, I will tell you that when Jesus' disciples asked *him* what they should pray about whenever they opened their mouths to pray (see Matthew 6), he didn't leave them high and dry. He told them what to pray! So yes, there is wisdom to be had in this regard. But we do well to remember the order of things: Context is greater than content as far as our prayer practice is concerned.

In terms of what Jesus instructed his disciples to pray—and by extension, you and me—there were seven key elements, as follows:

1. "Our Father in heaven" (Matthew 6:9): First, establish your relationship with God the Father. Tell him once more that you view him as your Father, your guardian, your guide.

2. "Hallowed be your name" (v. 9): Second, reaffirm your view of God's holiness, his "otherness." *Hallowed* simply means sacred. You honor God when you refer to him this way.

3. "Your kingdom come" (v. 10): Third, by saying to God, "Your kingdom come," you are saying "I anticipate the day when the entire earth surrenders to your authority in the same way I surrender to it now."

4. "Your will be done, on earth as it is in heaven" (v. 10): Similarly, this fourth element says to God, "I recognize that I have a will, and that it must be laid down in favor

of picking up yours. I make that choice today and thus receive with gratitude whatever you have for me now."

5. "Give us this day our daily bread" (v. 11): Fifth, tell God
   that you willfully look to him to provide for your needs
   instead of charging off in your own direction to try to
   fill them some other way. Our cups "runneth over," the
   ancient text from Psalm 23 promises, whenever we trust
   God, alone, to fill.

6. "And forgive us our debts as we also have forgiven our
   debtors" (v. 12): Sixth, as 1 John 1:9 instructs us to do,
   receive the forgiveness God has for you, and then pass that
   forgiveness along.

7. "And lead us not into temptation, but deliver us from evil"
   (v. 13): And finally, the seventh element is to confirm your
   commitment to loving the things God loves and hating all
   that he hates.

You probably noticed that, taken thematically, this model prayer
from Jesus includes an aspect of honoring and worshiping the Father, an aspect of welcoming both the wins and the woes in life,
an aspect of surrendering one's life to his will and ways, and an
aspect of anticipating all that is to come for those who are living
"in Christ." My dear friend the late Adrian Rogers, former pastor
of Bellevue Baptist Church in Memphis, Tennessee, took these four
primary themes and crafted the acrostic "PACE." A group of us
pastors who all treasured Dr. Rogers's mentorship in our lives were
meeting with him once when he shared this approach to prayer. I
never forgot it, and I look to it often. I hope it is useful to you as well.

P *is for Praise*

We praise God not only because he is *worthy* to be praised but
also because when we come to him with praise on our lips, that
posture sets the tone for everything else to come. You might say,

"You are holy, Father, and you are worthy of all my praise. I praise you now for your great power, which eclipses all other powers in this world."

Or, "I praise you, Father, for your presence, which accompanies me through life."

Or, "I praise you, Father, for your mercies, which are here to greet me afresh this day."

Or, "I praise you, Father, for your compassion, for your desire that *all* people would follow you."

Or, "I praise you, Father, for your unparalleled wisdom and that you're willing to share it with me."

Before you ask God to look upon the needs you've brought him, look upon his greatness and say what you see. Praising God first reminds us that regardless of the burdens we bear, this good, good Father of ours has purpose even despite our pain.

A *is for Accept*

Next, we accept whatever God has allowed into our life, whether the circumstances are dreadful or desired. We accept God's blessings. We accept the trials he will use to refine us. We accept the parts of life that are abundant, and we accept the parts that are scarce. We accept the sunshine, and we accept the rain. We receive all our Father desires to give, knowing that he is working things together for our good.

This sounds so simple, right? During my miserably melancholy months, acceptance was the hardest part of my day. I didn't want to be depressed. I wanted my old life back. And yet God clearly needed me to learn some things that only depression could teach. I remember being drawn to the book of Psalms during that season because the psalmist's sentiments were real and raw. One minute he would rage in anger over his circumstances, only to shift gears a few lines later and praise God for his goodness again. Now, *that* was an emotional state I could relate to.

I encouraged you in the last chapter to not merely read God's Word, but to pray through it, and if you're facing troubling circumstances, there is no better place to begin than in the book of Psalms. Select any psalm and then personalize it as a prayer from you to the Lord. An example, from Psalm 13: "How long, O LORD? Will you forget me forever? How long will you hide your face from me? How long must I take counsel in my soul and have sorrow in my heart all the day? How long shall my enemy, depression, be exalted over me? Consider and answer me, O LORD my God; light up my eyes, lest I sleep the sleep of death, lest my enemy say, 'I have prevailed over him,' lest this darkness and depression rejoice because I am shaken. But I have trusted in your steadfast love; my heart shall rejoice in your salvation. I will sing to the LORD, because he has dealt bountifully with me."

Many of the psalms, such as this one, paint a marvelous picture, both of the frenetic state we're in today and of the faithful state of surrender we long to return to. As I personalized and prayed those words, I was made aware of what I needed from God. For example, in my current state, I was fearful that darkness and depression really were going to overtake me, that I'd never gain victory over them. But then in my future state, echoing the psalmist's words, I really did want to trust in the Lord's "steadfast love." The question was how to get from here to there, how to move from *terror* to *trust*.

As I sat with that question in a posture of prayer, God began to remind me that if I had faith the size of even a mustard seed—just the *tiniest bit* of faith—then I could move mountains in my life. Depression sure felt like a mountain . . . was he saying I could move even that?

I figured it was worth a try and so I prayed for a little bit of faith. I prayed that my mountain would move.

My point is this: If you are having trouble accepting the challenges you're facing today, *ask God for what you need.*

Do you need patience to accept the circumstances in your life?

63

Do you need compassion to accept the circumstances in your life?

Do you need boldness to accept the circumstances in your life?

Like me, do you need faith to accept the circumstances in your life?

Do you need endurance?

Or perspective?

Or hope?

Or peace?

Ask God for what you need. "You do not have, because you do not ask," James 4:2 reminds us. Ask God for what you need so that your acceptance of that which he's appointed to you can unfold in your mind and heart.

Recently I received a text from a dear friend who has been enduring a trial in his life that has left him gutted. He said, "Pastor, I've never asked God why I'm having to go through all of this, but I have asked how long. How long will I have to stay in this furnace? How much more will he ask me to take?"

I will tell you the same thing I told him, the same thing I've had to tell myself: We don't know how long our trials will last, but we do know that God will be with us. And whatever will help us to stay the course, he stands ready to meet those needs. "Blessed is the man who remains steadfast under trial," James 1:12 says, "for when he has stood the test he will receive the crown of life, which God has promised to those who love him."

Bible teacher Warren Wiersbe used to say that whenever we are in the fire, God keeps his eye on the thermometer and his hand on the thermostat. God sees and knows how much and how long. And while it may seem unnecessarily harsh, it's the truth: The only ones who net the blessings of perseverance are those who persevere.

C *is for Commit*

Third, we reaffirm before God our commitment to live for him, devoting our thoughts, our attitudes, our words, our plans, our families, our friendships, our *everything* to him alone. Here is where we tell God, "I surrender to *your* will. I surrender to *your* ways. I surrender to *your* wisdom. I commit the sum of my life to you."[6]

A few years ago, I was asked to serve as the honorary chairman for the National Day of Prayer, an annual gathering on the first Thursday of May in our nation's capital and throughout the land that was established during the presidency of Harry S. Truman in 1952. Our theme that year was taken from 1 Kings 8:28 in which King Solomon asks God to "hear the cry" (NIV) of his people, to lovingly listen to their plea.

Solomon was dedicating to God the Temple that would house his presence when he asked God to hear his cry, which made me wonder, *What kind of cry can invoke the presence of the Lord?*

That must be some kind of cry; wouldn't you agree?

A single word came to mind: *humble*. The kind of cry that compels God to come near is a selfless, humble cry. "If my people, who are called by my name, will humble themselves and pray and seek my face and turn from their wicked ways," 2 Chronicles 7:14 affirms, "then I will hear from heaven, and will forgive their sin and will heal their land" (NIV).

If we will humble ourselves, then healing will be at hand.

And so we commit to God by elevating him and lowering ourselves—our will, our ways, our lives.

Earlier in Solomon's life, when he was being appointed as king, 1 Kings 3 says that the Lord appeared to Solomon in a dream by night and said, "Ask what I shall give you" (v. 5).

Solomon had just been handed the biggest promotion of his life. All the luxury, all the power, all the prestige he could hope for. And now a genie-in-a-bottle wish?

Whatever would Solomon wish for? More authority? More respect? More wealth? Here is what he said to God:

> "And now, O LORD my God, you have made your servant king in place of David my father, although I am but a little child. I do

not know how to go out or come in. And your servant is in the midst of your people whom you have chosen, a great people, too many to be numbered or counted for multitude. Give your servant therefore an understanding mind to govern your people, that I may discern between good and evil, for who is able to govern this your great people?"

vv. 7–9

Because it "pleased the Lord that Solomon had asked this," as verse 10 says, God replied favorably to Solomon that day. "And God said to him, 'Because you have asked this, and have not asked for yourself long life or riches or the life of your enemies, but have asked for yourself understanding to discern what is right, behold, I now do according to your word. Behold, I give you a wise and discerning mind, so that none like you has been before you and none like you shall arise after you. I give you also what you have not asked, both riches and honor, so that no other king shall compare with you, all your days. And if you will walk in my ways, keeping my statutes and my commandments, as your father David walked, then I will lengthen your days'" (vv. 10–14).

What is the lesson here? It is that when we commit our ways to the Lord—to his perspective, to his wisdom, to his path—we prevail, and there is no exception to this rule.

E is for Expect

Finally, we end our time with our gracious God in a posture of expectancy, of looking ahead to all that he has promised, to all that he will do, and to all that we will become.

Following my two-month sabbatical, I was cleared to preach again, and I'm not sure I've ever looked forward to a date on my calendar as much as I looked forward to that Sunday at church. September 13, 2009—that would be the day I would ascend the handful of stairs leading to the platform, set my Bible down on the pulpit, look out at the congregation I so deeply love, and say with a smile, "I'm baaaack!"

The text I preached from was Isaiah 40:29–31, which says, "He gives power to the faint, and to him who has no might he increases strength. Even youths shall faint and be weary, and young men shall fall exhausted; but they who wait for the LORD shall renew their strength; they shall mount up with wings like eagles; they shall run and not be weary; they shall walk and not faint."

What I reminded our congregation of that day is what I'll remind you of now: Although it's easy to focus on the lofty promises of a passage such as this one—the power, the strength, the endurance, the ability to take flight with the birds of the sky—we do well to focus instead on the impetus for these things, which is the injunction to "wait for the LORD."

During the year that I was battling depression, our entire country was battling recession, and to a person we were looking for answers. How did this happen? How would we survive? When on earth would it end? The fact was, we just didn't know. To quote Warren Wiersbe again: "We do not live by explanations; we live by promises."[7] So much of life cannot be explained. So much of life we simply accept.

As scores of my friends and congregants faced the loss of their life savings, the decimation of their 401(k) funds, wild drops in their housing values, and in many cases the shuttering of businesses they had started decades before, it was hard to know what to hope for, what to believe in, what to expect. Would the day really ever come when we would *mount up with wings like eagles*? Would we ever run again and not grow tired?

The answer, of course, was yes . . . so long as we waited on the Lord. Returning to God. Resting in God. Being delivered from our frantic selves. If we'd slow our pace and sit with him, our strength would be renewed.

I've preached nearly every Sunday for fifty years, since I was nineteen years old, and that sabbatical represented the longest stretch of time I'd ever been out of the pulpit. I'm telling you, it was *miserable*.

And yet, it was also *pure magnificence*. I still had many months to endure before the cloud of darkness fully dissipated, but already I'd experienced God ministering to me, there in the stillness, in the waiting, in the pit. In ways I couldn't detect until hindsight was on my side, God was refreshing my faith in his perfect timing, perfect ways, teaching me to trust him all over again.

One morning, when I was lying in bed feeling despondent, God brought to mind a powerful memory of a pivotal time in my life. It was the mid-1990s, and our church was situated on the corner of a busy intersection in North Dallas. We had been experiencing incredible growth as a congregation and now were jamming ourselves into a too-small building week after week. To complicate matters, we had limited parking, which meant we had to bus people from remote lots to the church's front doors for every service. It was a logistical nightmare.

As a leadership team, we had been patchworking solutions for years; most recently we'd drawn up plans for building a student center across the street where there was an empty parking lot, then installing sky bridges from that building to our church's main building so that students could walk instead of being bused back and forth. But was underbuilding our need yet again (not to mention overbuilding the neighborhood) really the best option? We weren't entirely sure.

Around that time, my family and I were enjoying a week of vacation in Colorado. I was out for a jog when I heard the powerful voice of God. I'm not sure if it was audible or not, but here is what he said: "Jack, you're limiting what I want to do with this church."

I wasn't sure what he meant, so I asked God. And he replied, "I have bigger plans for this church."

Bigger than our fancy sky bridge and adjunct student center? I had no clue what that could be.

Upon returning from vacation, I gathered my team and told them what I'd heard. We agreed to wait on the Lord.

Now, looking back, I can see what God was up to. In fact, as soon as we broke ground on our current campus, which is situated just a few miles northwest of that old building, I could see perfectly what he meant. But back then I could only wonder what would unfold. And yet God's guidance was unmistakable: *Stop what you're doing. I'm up to something greater here. Don't get ahead of me. Wait.*

I read the words of the prophet Isaiah today, and I can't help but smile. For many years, the other senior staff and I labored to push a boulder uphill. We were determined to make the old building work for us and we couldn't conceive of a different way. We were weary. We were exhausted. On *many* days, we felt faint. But there we were, rushing from solution to solution, rarely pausing to consult with God.

He gives power to the faint, the prophet promises.

He increases strength to those with no might.

He causes the weak to mount up like eagles.

He ensures that the runner will not grow faint.

And when does he tend to these objectives? When you and I willingly wait on him.

With hands lifted high, we *praise* God.

With palms turned upward to heaven, we *accept* the circumstances he has allowed.

With hands over our heart, we *commit* to his wisdom, his ways.

With arms outstretched before us, we *expect* the power and strength that will come.

We establish this PACE for ourselves, day after day, remembering that he is God and we are not.

3

Loving What Jesus Loves

The church is not a select circle of the immaculate, but a home where the outcast may come in. It is not a palace with gate attendants and challenging sentinels along the entrance-ways holding off at arm's length the stranger, but rather a hospital where the brokenhearted may be healed, and where all the weary and troubled may find rest and take counsel together.

James H. Aughey, *Spiritual Gems of the Ages*

Let us hold fast the confession of our hope without wavering, for he who promised is faithful. And let us consider how to stir up one another to love and good works, not neglecting to meet together, as is the habit of some, but encouraging one another, and all the more as you see the Day drawing near.

Hebrews 10:23–25

It goes down as one of the worst decisions I've ever made. True, the advice to make this decision had come to me via a trusted friend. But still, the decision had been mine, and the fact that I chose poorly is 100 percent on me. When the stakes in my life

71

were highest, instead of leaning into the support system God has surrounded me with since I was a little boy, I decided to go solo, leaving myself vulnerable to pain and attack.

By way of context, as I faced prostate surgery in the spring of 2009, I truly believed I would be fine. I knew this was a major operation—you can't just cut out parts of your body and expect everything to keep humming along—but I also knew I had a strong constitution and a work ethic that was even stronger. *Why bother the church with the details of my personal health?* I reasoned. *Who wants a sick pastor to worry about?* I tried to imagine myself explaining to the good people of Prestonwood that I'd received a troubling diagnosis and needed surgery to right some wrongs in my body, and in my mind's eye, whenever I got to the part where I had to say *cancer*, I pictured little children cowering in fear. The C word has a way of sucking all the air from a room, and the last thing I wanted to do was terrify our younger set. *I'll get through this and have a great story of God's faithfulness to share later on*, I decided. *That's the prudent thing to do.*

But then came the surgery. And the ensuing pathology report. And the surgeon's speculation: "Jack, I'm not confident that we got it all. . . ."

And the sleepless nights.

And the exhaustion.

And the anxiety.

And the twentieth-anniversary celebration that I was just barely present for.

And the fear.

And the depression.

And the unexpected two-month sabbatical that was necessitated by my inability to pull it together to preach.

The bottom line was that I needed God's people. I needed the lifeline of the church I loved.

Why the Church?

During Jesus' earthly ministry, he told his followers that in addition to coming to them in bodily form to testify to the truth (see John 18:37), he had come to build his Church. In Matthew 16:13–19, we read,

> Now when Jesus came into the district of Caesarea Philippi, he asked his disciples, "Who do people say the Son of Man is?" And they said, "Some say John the Baptist, others say Elijah, and others Jeremiah or one of the prophets." He said to them, "But who do you say that I am?" Simon Peter replied, "You are the Christ, the Son of the living God." And Jesus answered him, "Blessed are you, Simon Bar-Jonah! For flesh and blood has not revealed this to you but my Father who is in heaven. And I tell you, you are Peter, and on this rock I will build my church, and the gates of hell shall not prevail against it. I will give you the keys of the kingdom of heaven, and whatever you bind on earth shall be bound in heaven, and whatever you loose on earth shall be loosed in heaven."

When Jesus said that "on this rock" he would build his Church, he wasn't referring to building his Church on Peter (whose name means "rock"), as some would believe, but rather on the rock of the *confession of faith in him*, the Messiah. "Let us hold fast the confession of our hope without wavering," Hebrews 10:23 begins—"our hope" referring to the gospel of grace in Christ.

In other words, those who were "called out" from the world based on faith in Christ would come together as one body, one organism, to testify to the existence of Jesus, the uniqueness of Jesus, and the power to save that Jesus holds in his hands. In so doing, they would be fulfilling the Great Commission, the final marching orders that Jesus had left for the men, women, and children who believed in him. "All authority in heaven and on earth has been given to me," he said to his disciples in Galilee before he ascended back to the Father. "Go therefore and make disciples of all nations, baptizing them in the name of the Father and of the Son and of the Holy Spirit, teaching them to observe all that I have commanded you. And behold, I am with you always, to the end of the age" (Matthew 28:18–20).

The promise to "be with" us would be fulfilled with the impartation of the Holy Spirit, which John 14:23–26 beautifully lays out: "If anyone loves me, he will keep my word, and my Father will love him, and we will come to him and make our home with him. Whoever does not love me does not keep my words. And the word that you hear is not mine but the Father's who sent me. These things I have spoken to you while I am still with you. But the Helper, the Holy Spirit, whom the Father will send in my name, he will teach you all things and bring to your remembrance all that I have said to you."

The Church of Jesus Christ, then, was intended to be both *empowered*—by God's Spirit—and *empowering*, as its members took the message of grace that had revolutionized their lives to those in need of spiritual revolution themselves. This was far from a regular organization or institution. This was the living, breathing body of Christ at work down through the ages, in every people group imaginable, all across the world, a "colony of heaven in the country of death," as the late Eugene Peterson famously said.[1] And if you've ever been part of a local church that is healthy, then you know that his sentiment is right.

The big-C Church as Jesus envisioned it is not a farce but a force, not superficial but supernatural, not boring but transforming, not divided but unified. "All who believed were together and had all things in common," the apostle Luke wrote of the early church in Acts 2:44. Those who believed "were of one heart and soul, and no one said that any of the things that belonged to him was his own, but they had everything in common," Acts 4:32–35 confirms. "And with great power the apostles were giving their testimony to the resurrection of the Lord Jesus, and great grace was upon them all. There was not a needy person among them, for as many as were owners of lands or houses sold them and brought the proceeds of what was sold and laid it at the apostles' feet, and it was distributed to each as any had need."

Whenever I think about the selflessness and service, the participation and power, the commonality and unity of the Church, I remember the times when I've seen birds take to the sky in V formation, working in stunning synchrony to get where they're trying to go. One bird takes the tip of the V, fighting the wind on behalf of the others, and when that lead bird wearies, another takes his place so that he can draft at the back for a while. Every bird rotates through that key position, participating, leading, serving, helping, "ministering," if you will, to the rest of the flock. And together, those birds arrive safely at their destination—unharmed, unfettered, as one.

For the entirety of my life, it seems, I've been one of those birds. I've been upheld by the Church. I've been sustained by the Church. I've been enveloped in community by the Church. It has always been within the context of the Church that I've been taken to ever-new heights spiritually. I remember the sensation when I was a little boy of being so completely safe within the warm, caring community of my family's home church that during most Sunday night services, I'd lay my head in my mother's lap there in the pew and sleep through the entirety of our pastor's sermon. I remember learning the stories and singing the songs declaring the love of our heavenly Father. I remember surrendering my life to the lordship of Jesus when I was barely eight years old.

It was in the Church that I was discipled in the will and ways of our Father.

It was in the Church that I learned righteousness's path.

It was in the Church that I received my call into ministry.

It was in the Church that I married my bride.

It was in the Church that Deb and I raised our three children.

It was in the Church that all good things occurred.

And if I have one aspiration in life in terms of role and responsibilities, it is to help lead the Church toward our ultimate goal: people the world over bending a knee and proclaiming with passion that Jesus is Lord of all.

I love the Church.

I love gathering together as a Church.

I love the ministry of the saints in each other's lives.

In chapter 4, I'll explore the implications of isolating oneself from the Church, answering the question, "What's the big deal if I decide to just do my own thing?" But first, let's refresh our understanding on what the Church of Jesus Christ looks like when the Church is as she should be.

The Priorities of the Church

In the apostle Paul's letter to the believers gathered at Corinth, he confirmed that as it relates to the gathering of Jesus' Church, "all things should be done decently and in order" (1 Corinthians 14:40), which is why in many local churches still today, an "order of service" or an "order of worship" will be made plain. In terms of what that order ought to include, local churches down through the ages have taken their cues from Acts chapter 2: "And they [the believers composing the Church] devoted themselves to the apostles' teaching and the fellowship, to the breaking of bread and the prayers. . . . And day by day, attending the temple together and breaking bread in their homes, they received their food with glad and generous hearts, praising God and having favor with all the people. And the Lord added to their number day by day those who were being saved" (Acts 2:42, 46–47).

Preaching.

Teaching.

Learning the Word of God.

Praying together.

Singing worship songs to God.

Giving to those in need.

Sharing the Lord's Supper.

Sharing *life*.

And doing so, as Luke reminded us, with "glad and generous hearts" (v. 46).

The beliefs that united them—that there is "one body and one Spirit," according to Paul's words in Ephesians 4:4–6, "one Lord, one faith, one baptism, one God and Father of all, who is over all, through all and in all"—catalyzed unity in lifestyle too. This community of kindred spirits was advancing not a cause but a *kingdom*, all to the glory of God. In other words, there were no "free-range" believers. *One for all, and all for one*—that was more the approach. And how did that approach work? According to Acts 11, 13, 16, and 28, the early church spread like wildfire throughout Jerusalem, Judea, and Samaria to Antioch (today a town in Turkey), to Asia Minor (modern-day country of Turkey), to Macedonia (former contemporary Yugoslav Republic), to Greece, and to Rome. Later, it would blow through the entirety of the Roman Empire, seeing souls converted left and right, all in all taking a movement comprising twelve unknown men to the world's largest religion, numbering 2.3 billion souls.[2]

The secret sauce to the Church's success is *unity*. It's our togetherness. It's our "we." Which is why, for the fully surrendered follower of Jesus, the injunction found in Hebrews 10:24–25 is an absolutely *delightful* command to obey. "Let us consider how to stir up one another to love and good works," that passage says, "not neglecting to meet together, as is the habit of some, but encouraging one another, and all the more as you see the Day drawing near."

When you love sports, it's a blast to get together with other sports fans and take in a game.

When you love art, it's a joy to get together with other art lovers and meander through a gallery.

When you love good food, you want to get together with other foodies and relish an expertly crafted meal.

When you love movies, it's exciting to get together with other movie lovers for the release of what's sure to an award-winning film.

And when you love the Church, it's a joy to get together with other Church lovers to worship the risen Christ. Even if the Bible *didn't* command us to gather as the Church, the Church would gather with joy. Why? Because we recognize that all the good stuff that happens for believers *happens in the context of the Church*.

What kind of church can produce this kind of joy and commitment? Here are the characteristics of a holy and healthy church.

Jesus Is Loved and Celebrated

If there is one central confession of the Church of Jesus Christ, it is that Jesus is the Son of the living God and that he holds this role alone. He is not one among many; he is *other*, through and through. He is not a good man; he is the one true God-man—all God, all man. He is not the best way to heaven; he is the *only* way there is. "I am the way, and the truth, and the life," Jesus said to Thomas, who was worried that Jesus would be leaving the other disciples and him soon. "No one comes to the Father except through me" (John 14:6).

This upholding of Jesus as Lord is critical, because it is Jesus who builds his Church. Remember the passage we looked at earlier where Jesus confirmed this very fact to Simon Peter? "On this rock [the confession of our hope in Jesus Christ]," Jesus said, "I will build my church" (Matthew 16:18). Notice that Jesus didn't say, "I will build *your* church." Or even, "You will build *my* church."

Some wish that the Church were a democracy, but a theocracy is what it is. Jesus was clear here about where the responsibility for church building lies. *He* will build *his* Church; this burden is solely his. And so it is critical to find a local church where Jesus reigns supreme. His name must be revered. His authority must be welcomed. His presence must be honored. His example must be pursued. You and I were made to be worshipers, and a healthy church will ensure that Jesus is the worshiped One.

Inside every human heart exists a void, a vacuum, a yearning, a longing, a hole. We're creations looking for reconnection with our Creator, and worship satisfies that search. We'll spend an entire lifetime, some of us, trying to plug that hole, worshiping anything we can find. We'll find a love interest to worship. We'll find a career to worship. We'll find a brand name to worship. A sports team, a recreational activity, the acquisition of bigger and better homes or cars or vacations—truly, anything will do. We'll stick that thing up on a pedestal faster than you can say hallelujah and cross our fingers that it will somehow satisfy. But of course it never does. The reason the Church is so critical in the world is that it is the one and only group tasked with telling everyone what will actually satisfy.

In the story of Jesus' encounter on a hot, dusty day with the Samaritan woman at the well, he says to her, "Give me a drink" (John 4:7), to which the woman says, "How is it that you, a Jew, ask for a drink from me, a woman of Samaria?" (v. 9). In those days, Jews had "no dealings with Samaritans," and men had little use for women. Culturally speaking, this interaction simply shouldn't have occurred. Here is what Jesus said: "If you knew the gift of God, and who it is that is saying to you, 'Give me a drink,' you would have asked him, and he would have given you living water" (v. 10). The woman was baffled by this remark. He had nothing in hand with which to draw water. What on earth could he mean? "Everyone who drinks of this water will be thirsty again," Jesus told her, indicating the well, "but whoever drinks of the water that I will give him will never be thirsty again. The water that I will give him will become in him a spring of water welling up to eternal life" (vv. 13–14).

What Jesus was offering the Samaritan woman that day is what he offers us here and now: a cup of cool water that will never run dry. Satiety. Satisfaction. Life with our thirst forever quenched. I tell you, those of us who have had that cup filled can't *help* but celebrate. Which is precisely what worship ought to be. We're alive! We've been redeemed! We need never thirst again! We lift up the name of Jesus because we recognize that it's by his name that we've been saved.

The Word of God Is Proclaimed, Taught, Honored, and Believed

Second, to be considered healthy, churches must proclaim, teach, honor, and believe the holy Word of God. (And, I am quick to mention, this Book *alone*.) In 2 Timothy 4, the apostle Paul, writing to his protégé, Timothy, charges him "in the presence of God and of Christ Jesus, who is to judge the living and the dead, and by his appearing and his kingdom" to "preach the word; be ready in season and out of season; reprove, rebuke, and exhort, with complete patience and teaching" (vv. 1–2). Paul warns Timothy about the days ahead, saying, "The time is coming when people will not endure sound teaching, but having itching ears they will accumulate for themselves teachers to suit their own passions, and will turn away from listening to the truth and wander off into myths. . . . Always be sober-minded," Paul says, "endure suffering, do the work of an evangelist, fulfill your ministry" (vv. 3–5).

Proclaim God's Word.

Teach God's Word.

Honor God's Word.

Believe God's Word.

If these things aren't happening—continuously, enthusiastically, and with an attitude of complete surrender—in the church you're part of, then it's time for you to find another church.

Service Is Assumed

It is my belief that every person walking the planet today has a deep-seated desire to make a positive difference in the world. I'll concede the point that pathologies can and do exist, but I have found those to be the exception, not the norm. As a rule, people want to make the world a better place to live in. They want to contribute to that which is worthwhile and impactful, beautiful and good. This is why it is generally so refreshing for new believers to come upon the words of Ephesians 2:8–10. "For by grace you have been saved through faith," that passage reads. "And this is not your own doing; it is the gift of God, not a result of works, so that no one may boast. For we are his workmanship, created in Christ Jesus for good works, which God prepared beforehand, that we should walk in them."

If you track with Paul's logic here, then you'll see that he is careful to confirm that while we are not saved *by* good works, we certainly are saved for them. And based on countless thousands of testimonies I have heard around the world, the surest and swiftest way to open the gifts God has left in our path is to drape a towel over the arm and *serve*. Serving God by loving others, utilizing each of your spiritual gifts, is what makes your church experience meaningful ministry.

"You have not lived today until you have done something for someone who can never repay you," the late, great preacher and writer of *The Pilgrim's Progress*, John Bunyan, is quoted as having said. He's right, you know. Serving is a day-maker every time.

People Are Coming to Faith

Want a fourth sign of local-church health? It's that *people are coming to faith*. Seems obvious, I know, but you might be surprised by how many churches exist in our world that make Jesus ridiculously difficult to find.

People around Prestonwood know that our mission is to glorify God by introducing Jesus Christ as Lord to as many people as possible and to develop them in Christian living using the most effective means to impact the world, making an eternal difference in this generation. How do we do this? By pointing *every ministry effort* toward reaching those in our neighborhoods and around the world who have yet to come to faith in Jesus Christ. We make sure that in every gathering, a public invitation is given to allow people to respond to the clear message of hope and eternal promise found in the Lord Jesus Christ. Further, we challenge every member of the church to share their faith daily in work, at school, and in social settings, so that people in their individual spheres of influence might come to know the Lord.

In my experience, churches are either helping people to find faith in Jesus and mature in him or they aren't. Given the commission we've been given, I can think of no higher aim than to do what Jesus has asked us to do: find people in need of rescue and make disciples of Jesus Christ. We must remember that the church exists for people not yet in it! Which leads us to the fifth sign of a healthy church—namely, that ministry never stops.

Ministry Never Stops

A fifth and final sign of church health is that ministry persists.

If there is a better picture of what it looks like to thrive as the body of Christ than the one offered in the second half of James 1, I don't know what it is. By way of context, the apostle James wrote the book to encourage early believers in their faith. He wanted to exhort them not only to be hearers of the word but also doers of it, to back up their words with action:

> But be doers of the word, and not hearers only, deceiving yourselves. For if anyone is a hearer of the word and not a doer, he is like a man who looks intently at his natural face in a mirror. For he looks at himself and goes away and at once forgets what he was like. But the one who looks into the perfect law, the law of liberty, and perseveres, being no hearer who forgets but a doer who acts, he will be blessed in his doing.

If anyone thinks he is religious and does not bridle his tongue but deceives his heart, this person's religion is worthless. Religion that is pure and undefiled before God the Father is this: to visit orphans and widows in their affliction, and to keep oneself unstained from the world.

James 1:22–27

A church that is surrendered to the lordship of Jesus and committed to helping its members look and live and lead more like him prioritizes the three outcomes James references. They equip their people to develop a *controlled tongue*, a *compassionate heart*, and a *consecrated life*.

A controlled tongue. Healthy churches model controlled speech. They understand that words matter. That emotions matter. That what people say—and how they say it—can lead listeners toward the person of Jesus or repel them fast. And so they elevate these practices James mentions, being quick to hear, being slow to speak, being slow to anger, being careful to put away filthy speech, being committed to rightly handling God's Word.

A compassionate heart. Healthy churches foster in their people hearts of compassion. Listen, while I deeply regret keeping the events surrounding my cancer diagnosis and prostate surgery hidden from my congregation until those events had come and gone, I have to tell you that the moment I did stand in the pulpit and come clean about the trials I was working through, *not one person* rebuked me for my deception—at least, not to my face. Instead, my church came around me and enfolded me in love and heartfelt concern. We don't get everything right around Prestonwood, but that reflexive, compassionate response told me all I needed to know about the culture of our church. Compassion, not judgment or anger toward, but rather *earnest concern* for another's misfortunes, is a leading indicator of healthfulness—in a person, in a family, in a church.

A consecrated life. Healthy churches encourage their people to live fully consecrated lives. To consecrate something is to dedicate it to a higher purpose, to mark it as holy, to set it apart. For spiritual people, this means staying in step with the Spirit we serve: the third person of the Trinity, the Holy Spirit, the Spirit of God.

Because the apostle Paul laid out for us in his letter to the church at Galatia what it looks like and sounds like and feels like when Christ followers live spiritually "in step," it is easy to discern whether a church is following suit. Here is what he said:

> But I say, walk by the Spirit, and you will not gratify the desires of the flesh. For the desires of the flesh are against the Spirit, and the desires of the Spirit are against the flesh, for these are opposed to each other, to keep you from doing the things you want to do. But if you are led by the Spirit, you are not under the law. Now the works of the flesh are evident: sexual immorality, impurity, sensuality, idolatry, sorcery, enmity, strife, jealousy, fits of anger, rivalries, dissensions, divisions, envy, drunkenness, orgies, and things like these. I warn you, as I warned you before, that those who do such things will not inherit the kingdom of God. But the fruit of the Spirit is love, joy, peace, patience, kindness, goodness, faithfulness, gentleness, self-control; against such things there is no law. And those who belong to Christ Jesus have crucified the flesh with its passions and desires.
>
> If we live by the Spirit, let us also keep in step with the Spirit. Let us not become conceited, provoking one another, envying one another.
>
> Galatians 5:16–26

In a healthy church, the *typical tendency* is for its people to encourage each other toward the good list, not the bad. As a normal course of action, believers are spurred on to pursue the patient response, the loving action, the joyful perspective, the gentle approach. They are prompted to follow Jesus' example, who described himself in Matthew 11:29 as "gentle and lowly in heart."

You and the Church

So far, we've spent the entirety of this chapter talking about the Church's responsibility for healthfulness, and that onus is properly placed. But it's important to remember that the Church can't be the Church without the people who make it up—namely you, and me, and every other believer alive today. While we tend to refer to the Church as a building ("Let's go to church") or an institution ("We were married by the Church"), in fact, the Church is people, it's believers . . . it's *us*. So here are three questions for you to uncover the onus *you* bear.

Am I Showing Up?

Let me engage you in a quick thought experiment. Suppose you came up to me and said, "Hey, Jack, I'd really like to have you over for dinner. When are you free?" And then I said, "How nice! Let me check with Deb and get back to you." And then you said, "Oh, the invitation is just for you. I don't like Deb. I just like you."

Do you think I'm going to accept your dinner invitation?

If you like Jesus, then you also like his Church. Further, you will show up for his Church—first, by literally just *showing up*.

According to a survey from 2019, 23 percent of Americans attend church every week—just under one in four. More depressing still, 29 percent—about one in three—reported that they never went to church.[3] My guess is that for the 23 percent who attend every week, they have habitualized this act. They don't wake up on Sunday mornings and ask, "Hmm, do I feel like going to church today?" No, somewhere along the way, they predecided that church would be part of their weekly routine, so now each weekend they rest in the fact that their choice has already been made. There's a lesson for all believers here. If you want to reignite your faith, then recommit yourself to Jesus' Church. Say yes to meeting together, as Hebrews 10:25 counsels us to do. And then let your yes be yes—simple as that—week after week.

Two things will happen for you once you put your church-attendance stake in the ground. First, you will begin to feel connected. You'll see familiar faces time and again. Someone will remember your name, and that will make you feel seen. You'll begin to arrive a few minutes early and stay a few minutes late, talking with the people who were kind enough to talk to you, getting to know them, bit by bit.

You'll receive an invitation to help out with something one weekend, and despite your initial concerns about stepping into the world of service, you'll hear yourself saying, "Sure."

You'll be invited to join a small group, and again you'll give it a try.

You'll know more about what's going on in the life of the church because you'll be there to hear things announced. And step by step, you'll avail yourself of the opportunities you're given to learn, to serve, to grow.

The few people you have met and come to know will introduce you to a few people they know, and you'll find that your relational sphere has quickly doubled. Those folks will introduce you to their people, and that sphere will double again. Now you can't even walk through the church doors without someone hollering, "Hey, Joe! Good to see you!"

"Hey, Alison!"

"Hey, Jacob!"

"Hey, Claire!"

There's something about the sound of our own name, isn't there? It is the sweetest sound there is. Those initial greetings will morph into earnest conversations: questions asked, prayers prayed, meals shared. "We are not just hungry bodies, nor machines that simply need fuel," writes Justin Whitmel Earley in his book *The Common Rule*. "We are hungry souls; we are people who crave the company and the delights of the table."[4]

You keep at this church-attendance thing, and before you know it, your soul will be hungry no more. You'll experience spiritual satiety, a certain filling from the inside out.

But there's a second thing that will happen as you commit to showing up for your church: You will become the conduit for others getting connected as this venture becomes less about you. You will be the one initiating conversation. You will be the one remembering names. You will be the one extending invitations to lunch. You will be the one praying fervent prayers. Remembering how it felt to be the newcomer, the outsider, the untethered one in the room, you will extend a hand of friendship and envelop *new* ones with care. And in doing these things, you will be acting as the hands and feet of Jesus, who longs for none to feel lonely, who longs for all to be welcome in him.

Dr. Vivek Murthy served as our country's nineteenth surgeon general from 2014 to 2017, and by his own admission he expected that his role would encompass dealing with issues such as "obesity, tobacco-related disease, mental health, and vaccine-preventable illness," as he wrote in his book *Together: The Healing Power of Human Connection in a Sometimes Lonely World.*[5] What he did not anticipate was that the vast majority of the societal scourges he worked on remedying—the diabetic patient's looming amputation, the at-home mom's opioid addiction, the high school sophomore's consistent overeating—could be traced to a far more insidious disease still: loneliness. Murthy writes: "So many of the problems we face as a society—from addiction and violence to disengagement among workers and students to a political polarization—are worsened by loneliness and disconnection. Building a more connected world holds the key to solving these and many more of the personal and societal problems confronting us today."[6]

Despite our vast technological connectedness today, many believe that a "loneliness epidemic" is encircling the globe. "Imagine a condition," writes prolific social-research pair J. Holt-Lunstad and T. B. Smith, "that makes a person irritable, depressed, and self-centered, and is associated with a 26% increase in the risk of premature mortality. Imagine too that in industrialised countries around a third of people are affected by this condition, with one person in 12 affected severely, and that these proportions are increasing. Income, education, sex, and ethnicity are not protective, and the condition is contagious. The effects of the condition are not attributable to some peculiarity of the character of a subset of individuals, they are a result of the condition affecting ordinary people. Such a condition exists—loneliness."[7]

One in three of us suffers diagnosable loneliness—one in twelve severely so. Which means that as you make your way through life—running errands, connecting with friends and family members, reaching out to an elderly loved one, and yes, attending church—your mere presence in another's life provides powerful ministry. This is the salve of showing up.[8]

Am I Leaning In?

A second question for your consideration: *Am I leaning in?*

In the gospel of Mark, chapter 10, an interesting discussion arises. James and John, two of Jesus' disciples, had approached Jesus to ask about their position in the future scheme of things. Essentially, they wanted to be sure that in eternity, they'd have primo access to the King. "Grant us to sit, one at your right hand and one at your left, in your glory," they said to him (v. 37), to which Jesus replied by reminding them what his kingdom was like. "You know that those who are considered rulers of the Gentiles lord it over them, and their great ones exercise authority over them. But it shall not be so among you. But whoever would be great among you must be your servant, and whoever would be first among you must be slave of all. For even the Son of Man came not to be served but to serve, and to give his life as a ransom for many" (vv. 42–45).

Whenever I hear churchgoers complain about the church they're going to, grumbling that the music is too repetitive or the drums are too loud or the Sunday school classrooms are too dated or the pastor always goes long or the coffee isn't fresh or the carpet needs to be replaced or the drop-off spot is always clogged with people taking forever to unload, I can't help but think of that verse. *Are they at church to serve or to be served?* I wonder. *Have they come to believe it's all about them?*

Now, speaking as someone who works for the Church, I am convinced that the majority of pastors and church leaders want our places of worship to be immaculate, our worship gatherings to be excellent, and our systems to run as smoothly as they can. But to expect 100 percent perfection on these fronts is to sign up for a sure letdown. Instead of griping and grumbling, grab a towel, bend a knee, and serve. Something probably needs cleaning. Something probably needs organizing. Somebody probably needs mentoring. Somebody probably needs care. So, yes, while it matters deeply that you show up for your church, it matters every bit as much that you serve. Lean *into* the problems you see in your church. Lean *into* the holes you can fill. Lean *into* the issues you might help to resolve. Lean in instead of turning away.

"For by the grace given to me I say to everyone among you not to think of himself more highly than he ought to think," the apostle Paul wrote to believers gathered at the church of Rome, "but to think with sober judgment, each according to the measure of faith that God has assigned. For as in one body we have many members, and the members do not all have the same function, so we, though many, are one body in Christ, and individually members one of another. Having gifts that differ according to the grace given to us, let us use them: if prophecy, in proportion to our faith; if service, in our serving; the one who teaches, in his teaching; the one who exhorts, in his exhortation; the one who contributes, in generosity; the one who leads, with zeal; the one who does acts of mercy, with cheerfulness" (Romans 12:3–8).

If you're good at teaching, then teach! The Church needs sound teachers just like you.

If you're naturally an encourager, then encourage! The Church needs encouragers just like you.

If you've always been told you have the gift of leadership, then lead! The Church needs leaders just like you.

If you're good at project management, or organizing papers and files, or building production scenery, or creating compelling backgrounds for worship, or writing curricula, or explaining complex topics to children in simplified ways, or managing budgets, or singing, or dancing, or creating apps, or designing websites, or any of ten thousand other things, then bring those talents and skills and desires inside the community known as the Church.

The gifts God has given to us are not toys to play with, but tools to work with in building the Church. We can't fully grow up and grow stronger in the Lord unless and until we employ our spiritual gifts. And it is in the context of the Church that those gifts are discovered and most effectively put to use.

The Church is a body, the apostle Paul reminded us in his letter to the Corinthian church, that consists not of one member but of many. "If the foot should say, 'Because I am not a hand, I do not belong to the body,' that would not make it any less a part of the body. And if the ear should say, 'Because I am not an eye, I do not belong to the body,' that would not make it any less a part of the body. If the whole body were an eye, where would be the sense of hearing? If the whole body were an ear, where would be the sense of smell? But as it is, God arranged the members in the body, each one of them, as he chose. If all were a single member, where would the body be? As it is, there are many parts, yet one body" (1 Corinthians 12:15–20).

It takes all of us, in other words, to keep the body alive and vibrant, functioning to its fullest, most beautiful potential. It takes you and me leaning in.

Am I Holding Fast to Hope?

It has only been in the past two weeks that Prestonwood has been allowed by our state and local officials to reopen our campus to live, in-person worship services in the midst of the pandemic. For a dozen straight weekends, we held services via technology, which meant I preached to an empty sanctuary while families watched from home. It wasn't optimal; a preacher's nightmare is preparing a sermon for which nobody shows up. But we made do. Why? Because even if we must gather virtually, the Church will gather still. "We are in this together," I kept reminding our church family. "And even without access to our various buildings, the Church remains the Church. We are tens of thousands of points of light, scattered across this region. And while theme parks and city parks and restaurants and coffee shops and businesses and health clubs are closed for now, guess what is still wide open? The Church of Jesus Christ."

The Church will always be operational.

The Church will never close.

This is the hope that we have in this gathering, which is that because we are a body and not a building, and because the risen Lord is our head, we will never see the Church's demise. The Church will *always* prevail.

It is said that our nation's twenty-eighth president, Woodrow Wilson, who served in the role from 1913 until 1921, stated that he would rather fail in a cause that will ultimately succeed than succeed in a cause that will ultimately fail. As it relates to our involvement with the Church of Jesus Christ, we can rest assured that ultimate success is ours. Jesus *will* build his Church. The forces of hell will *not* prevail against it. Barriers will no longer exist between earth and heaven. And you and I can see that it's so.

4

Living from Victory

If we can infer anything from the body of the risen Jesus, it seems our scars are the only thing we get to take with us into eternity. Maybe it's so that when we've been dead for ten billion years and those few moments we had back on earth seem like a dream, we'll be able to say, "Yes, I really did live in that place of skid marks and scars. Yes, he really did come down and die in my place. Yes, I really did believe in him and he really did rise again. Yes, his love really did bring me here."

Steven James, *Story*

Let no one say when he is tempted, "I am being tempted by God," for God cannot be tempted with evil, and he himself tempts no one. But each person is tempted when he is lured and enticed by his own desire. Then desire when it has conceived gives birth to sin, and sin when it is fully grown brings forth death.

James 1:13–15

I was absentmindedly flipping channels waiting for both baseball games I was watching to come back from commercial break when I caught sight of a pack of elephants tromping through the tall grass of the African savanna, looking delighted to be enjoying the sunshine and warmth. But the ominous music track cued me that something nefarious was afoot. Baseball or not, I had to stick around to find out what was about to go down.

Of the dozen or so elephants on the screen, two were calves, and as the throng made its way across the plains, those babies would tuck themselves away into the center of the group. But when the herd stopped to graze, a flock of white birds scuttling around on the ground caught one calf's attention, and off the little guy went in search of the chase, pining for some adventure, craving a taste of independence from his group. A few moments later, after the birds took to the air once more, the baby elephant realized how far he had roamed from his pack. He stuck his little trunk up into the air and blew a weak, stuttering trumpet, which was likely what alerted the nearby pride of lions that dinner was being served.

As the elephant herd started moving again, the calf bumbled his way back toward the fold. But before he could get there, the lions made their move. Now the music really got intense as a hulking bull elephant ran frantically around the herd, trumpeting warnings and kicking up dust. The calf's mama made a beeline for her baby while seemingly yelling at the other mamas to gather round. The big bull squared off against the lions while the females stood their ground, and in the end the lions retreated, figuring they'd go pick an easier fight. The calf was spared, the herd safe, and the elephants continued on their path.[1]

Whew. Now back to baseball.

In the last three chapters, I walked us through the three primary practices in the life of a believer—immersion in the Word of God, faithfulness to prayer, and commitment to a local church—all for the purpose of making this point: Devoting yourself to Scripture, and to prayer, and to the body of Christ isn't just a nice habit to establish or a worthwhile thing to check off your daily list of to-do's. It is the *primary means for winning the battles* you and I both will face as we engage in this thing called life.

The book of 1 Peter was written by the apostle Peter to Jewish Christians who were scattered among the Gentiles outside of Palestine, and his central message was a straightforward one: *Stand firm*. Stand firm in your trials. Stand firm in your tribulations. Stand firm as opposition mounts. Stand firm, knowing God will provide. "I have written briefly to you," he confirmed in 1 Peter 5:12, "exhorting and declaring that this is the true grace of God. Stand firm in it."

The "this" Peter is referring to is Christianity, the "way of Christ." In essence he was encouraging them to cling to their followership of Jesus instead of being swayed by Judaism, by paganism, or by any other "ism" they cared to find. But it's the preceding comments Peter made to the Diaspora that I want to focus on here, found in chapter 5, verses 1 through 11:

> So I exhort the elders among you, as a fellow elder and a witness of the sufferings of Christ, as well as a partaker in the glory that is going to be revealed: shepherd the flock of God that is among you, exercising oversight, not under compulsion, but willingly, as God would have you; not for shameful gain, but eagerly; not domineering over those in your charge, but being examples to the flock. And when the chief Shepherd appears, you will receive the unfading crown of glory. Likewise, you who are younger, be subject to the elders. Clothe yourselves, all of you, with humility toward one another, for "God opposes the proud but gives grace to the humble."
>
> Humble yourselves, therefore, under the mighty hand of God so that at the proper time he may exalt you, casting all your anxieties on him, because he cares for you. Be sober-minded; be watchful. Your adversary the devil prowls around like a roaring lion, seeking someone to devour. Resist him, firm in your faith, knowing that the

same kinds of suffering are being experienced by your brotherhood throughout the world. And after you have suffered a little while, the God of all grace, who has called you to his eternal glory in Christ, will himself restore, confirm, strengthen, and establish you. To him be the dominion forever and ever. Amen.

Remember, Peter addressed these remarks to believers as a group, not as individuals, and in doing so imagined a compelling picture of the Church. Wise oversight, eagerness to serve, godly leadership, a fitting example to all, submission of younger to older, clothed in humility, carefulness to trust our heavenly Father, watchfulness at all times—this is the Church when the Church is working right. This is the Church we still can be. And why is such a church so critical? *Because we are all fighting spiritual battles.*

"Your adversary the devil prowls around like a roaring lion," Peter wrote (v. 8), "seeking someone to devour." Leaving very little to the imagination, Peter tells us that Satan is the beast skulking through the tall grasses, waiting for the independent renegade to gain just enough distance from the safety of his pack before he licks his chops. Dinner is served.

Contrary to popular opinion, it is not God who malevolently waits for us to trip and fall, cheering as we splat to the ground. "Let no one say when he is tempted, 'I am being tempted by God,' for God cannot be tempted with evil, and he himself tempts no one," James 1:13–15 says. "But each person is tempted when he is lured and enticed by his own desire. Then desire when it has conceived gives birth to sin, and sin when it is fully grown brings forth death." No, it is we who do it to *ourselves* by leaving ourselves wide open to opposition. And the opposition Satan delivers is nothing we want to see.

The big deal about my not asking God for input or being honest with myself or disclosing the truth of my burdensome situation to my church, back when I knew that cancer and all its awful trappings were going to be my reality for a while, was this: When we isolate and insulate and cut ourselves off from the protection God has ordained for us, we make ourselves needlessly vulnerable to attack. We give Satan ground we may never get back.

I think of the addict who one day doesn't show up for his church's Tuesday-night recovery meeting and quickly tumbles headlong into the pit from which he was trying to emerge.

I think of the couple who cancels the counseling appointment with their pastor and heads straight to filing for divorce.

I think of the woman sitting at her Wednesday-morning Bible study table group, knowing she would be helped tremendously by confiding in these women the truth of the affair she's been having but choosing to paint on a cheerful face during prayer-request time, convince them that everything is "great," climb back into her car once the meeting is over, and head off to Target instead.

I think of the man struggling with a pornography habit who walks by his Bible every morning and is tempted to pause but instead moves on.

I think of the self-hatred-filled teenager who watches through his bedroom window as his parents back out of the driveway on a Sunday morning to head to church while he pulls the covers over his head. "Losers," he mutters under his breath.

I think of the corporate executive who has become so stressed out and exhausted that he's finding it increasingly difficult to control his rage. Prayer would help. Of course it would. But who has time for that?

I think of the homeowner facing foreclosure who tossed the flyer from his church into the trash, the one advertising a financial-management class.

I think of all these people—myself included—and thousands more whose stories they've told me as tears sprang to their eyes, and I think, *If only you—if only we—had leaned into the prowess, the protection, the power God has for us! We could have avoided so much pain.*

I'm going to show you my cards early in this chapter: Satan and his band of fools ease in and out of our collective circles, watching, listening, filing away clues, so that when the moment is just right, they can pounce. A whispered lie. A baseless threat. A nudge toward the worldly priorities we used to prize. The plays in their playbook aren't exactly novel ("steal, kill, destroy"—that's it, according to John 10:10), but boy, can they mess us up. Thankfully, however, we have a choice. Yes, we can make their mission far easier by continuously stepping outside of the protective covering God has offered us. But equally true is this: We can make their work next to *impossible* by living wise to their ways. If you need a reignited faith, then recommit to reading your Bible. Return to prayer. Connect with and plug into a local church. But as you do so, remember this critical fact: *You and I are in a war.*

Ways We Play into the Enemy's Hands

Four summers ago, I released a book titled *Angels: Who They Are, What They Do, and Why It Matters,* and in my research for that work, I was refreshed in my understanding that while Satan and his demons have incredible, albeit temporary, power throughout the earth, they are incapable of the capacities that our heavenly Father possesses, such as reading our minds, knowing our intentions, and being everywhere at the same time. In 1 Kings 8, Solomon offers to God a prayer of dedication of the Temple. Solomon recounts the vast goodness of God, praising God for his inability to be contained, for his righteousness and sense of justice, for his quickness to forgive, and for his kindness in teaching his people his ways. And then he says this: "If there is famine in the land, if there is pestilence or blight or mildew or locust or caterpillar, if their enemy besieges them in the land at their gates, whatever plague, whatever sickness there is, whatever prayer, whatever plea is made by any man or by all your people Israel, each knowing the affliction of his own heart and stretching out his hands toward this house, then hear in heaven your dwelling place and forgive and act and render to each whose heart you know, according to all his ways (for you, you only, know the hearts of all the children of mankind)" (vv. 37–39).

Later, the words of Psalm 139 confirm God's deep knowledge of his creations' inner lives: "O LORD, you have searched me and known me! You know when I sit down and when I rise up; you discern my thoughts from afar. You search out my path and my lying down and are acquainted with all my ways. Even before a word is on my tongue, behold, O LORD, you know it altogether. You hem me in, behind and before, and lay your hand upon me. Such knowledge is too wonderful for me; it is high; I cannot attain it" (vv. 1–6).

In the first of the four gospel accounts, Jesus healed a man suffering from paralysis, saying, "Take heart, my son; your sins are forgiven" (Matthew 9:2), to which many of the scribes and religious leaders present muttered to themselves, "This man is blaspheming" (v. 3). "But Jesus," verse 4 reports, "*knowing their thoughts*, said, 'Why do you think evil in your hearts?'" (emphasis added).

In John 2:23–25, we read that when Jesus was "in Jerusalem at the Passover Feast, many believed in his name when they saw the signs that he was doing. But Jesus on his part did not entrust himself to them, because he knew all people and needed no one to bear witness about man, for he himself knew what was in man."

A few chapters later, Jesus explained to a gathered crowd that he was the Bread of Life, a claim that drew criticism from many and caused disputes about its meaning from the rest—"What does he mean he is 'bread' . . . are we to somehow eat his flesh?" When many of Jesus' disciples heard the dissension, some of them agreed. "But Jesus," John 6:61–64 says, "knowing in himself that his disciples were grumbling about this, said to them, 'Do you take offense at this? Then what if you were to see the Son of Man ascending to where he was before? It is the Spirit who gives life;

the flesh is no help at all. The words that I have spoken to you are spirit and life. But there are some of you who do not believe.' (For Jesus knew from the beginning who those were who did not believe, and who it was who would betray him.)"

A final point—this one having to do with Satan himself. In Isaiah 14, we learn that Satan fell from heaven upon determining in his heart to "set his throne on high" (v. 13). And while his aspirations were lofty, his plan was destined to fail. "But you are brought down to Sheol," verse 15 reads, "to the far reaches of the pit."

Utter destruction is irrevocably certain, which is kind of the exact opposite of what Satan hoped for. And yet still he won't give up the fight.

My message here is twofold. The first part is this: Satan is not God and as such does not have the power that God has. In other words, 100 percent of his intelligence regarding you and how to trip you up comes from what you say and how you behave. He can't know our thoughts until we translate them into words. He can't know our hearts until we act on our desires. And because he is confined by time and space, he can't assault you or me at the same time he's assaulting someone else. That's the good news. And while I won't go so far as to call the other part "bad news," it is sobering news indeed: Unless you and I stay crystal clear on the war that's being waged day by day for our souls, we will play right into Satan's evil scheme for our lives. We'll give him inches that he'll turn into miles.

So what does it look like for us to give Satan ground in our lives? I've thought long and hard about this—an occupational hazard, you might say, given the countless hours I've spent absorbing people's heart-wrenching tales of sinfulness and strife—and what I see rise to the surface nearly every time is one of three fatal flaws: distraction, deception, or compromise. I'll share my thoughts on each.

Living Distracted

I probably don't have to make a case for you regarding how distracted we all are today. If you can be alive in our twenty-first century reality and *not* feel like one of Pavlov's hyper-conditioned, experimental dogs that responds reflexively to every technological ping, ding, vibration, and bell, then I'd love to know your trick. Most of us simply aren't that self-controlled. And while we chuckle over our inability to stay focused, a laughing matter it is not.

What are we so distracted by? Here are the ones that top my list.

Distracted by Striving

We are distracted by desire. By striving. By wanting, by *craving* that thing—whatever that thing happens to be. We want the job. We want the diploma or degree. We want the house, and then the bigger, better house. We want the object of our addiction, be it pornography, gambling, drugs, or booze. We want the relationship, and then the more exciting, enticing relationship. We want the award. The accolade. The promotion. But will we be satisfied, even if we get the thing we so desire?

Regarding the thesis of his book *Stumbling on Happiness*, Harvard psychologist Daniel Gilbert speaks of the "two errors" we humans often make when contemplating the things we firmly believe will make us happy. The first error, he says, is that we "don't imagine events correctly." He explains: "We underestimate the mind's ability to react to events in a different way than it's reacting to them in prospect. . . . Almost every event you experience feels different once you've experienced it than you imagined it would have beforehand. That's the part of our psychology we don't seem very good at anticipating."[2]

You dread the business meeting that winds up going well.

You eagerly anticipate the vacation that leaves you exhausted and annoyed.

You look forward to seeing an old colleague and then struggle to find anything to talk about.

You almost bow out of the conference that delivers a defining moment for you.

The second—and more troublesome—error, according to Gilbert, is this: "We don't know who we will be when we are experiencing that event." In one telling study Gilbert and an associate of his conducted, they asked eighteen-year-olds to tell them how much they would change over the coming decade—between when they were age eighteen and age twenty-eight—and asked a group of twenty-eight-year-olds to say how much they had changed over the decade that had just passed since they themselves had been eighteen. "In a perfectly rational world," Gilbert said, "those numbers would be the same." And yet the results weren't at all the same. The eighteen-year-olds believed "they would change very little," even as the twenty-eight-year-olds admitted to "having changed a lot."[3]

"Why do you spend your money for that which is not bread," the prophet Isaiah recorded God as saying in Isaiah 55, "and your labor for that which does not satisfy? Listen diligently to me, and eat what is good, and delight yourselves in rich food. Incline your ear, and come to me; hear, that your soul may live; and I will make with you an everlasting covenant, my steadfast, sure love for David" (vv. 2–3).

In other words: *Quit being distracted, you who say you love me, with the things of this world. They will never do the trick for you.*

Distracted by Success

What about those times when we *do* get what we've been striving for? Just as we are poor judges of anticipating what will make us happy, we are also poor judges of how well we will behave once we acquire that supposed happiness-inducing thing. "God," we plead, "if you will just help me get this _____ (fill in the blank), then I will be *so faithful* to steward it well! Try me! You'll see. . . ."

Suffice it to say, a full cup is hard to carry without spilling—ask anyone whose cup has been full.

Distracted by Sulking

And then there are the times when we don't get what we've been striving for, and discouragement and fear set in. What a distraction *that* can be.

The predominant fear that racked me ten years ago was that the depression I was dealing with would never be dealt with in full, that I would never be made well. I walked around like that baby llama from the children's book who asked every animal it came across, "Are you my mama?" But my question was, "Am I going to be okay?"

I'd come across people who also had struggled with depression and ask, "Do you think I'm going to be okay?"

I'd ask trusted friends, "Will I ever be okay?"

I'd ask family members, "Are you sure I'll be okay?"

I'd ask anyone and everyone, it seemed, "What if I'm not ever okay again?"

I simply couldn't believe that the weight on my chest would lift, that I'd have another energized day, that life would feel joyful once more, that joy could possibly refill my soul. I feared I'd be depressed forever, that I'd never be "up" again. This is, incidentally, how you can detect a spirit of sulking in your life: Simply follow your fears. We fear that God won't ever again give us good things, because he didn't give us *this* good thing, and in light of that realization, we sulk. We don't use that word much anymore, but we ought to. It's a good one. To sulk is to mope. To fret. To grumble and groan and huff. It's the posture that looks heavenward and says, "Clearly, you're not paying attention or you'd *do something about this down here.*"

Distracted by Fear

During the pandemic that swept around the world in 2019 and 2020, for three months straight not a day went by when at least a handful of people didn't confide in me their fear.

What's more, partway through the pandemic's peak in most major cities, those places were overrun by protestors and, in some cases, violent aggressors over the brutal, unjust murder of George Floyd in Minneapolis.

The effect of these two burdens unfolding simultaneously was about as much as our collective conscience could hold, and questions outpaced answers in a flash. "When will we get back to normal?" "How do we get back to normal?" "What does normal mean, anyway?" "Do we even want to return to normal when 'normal' was such a terrible reality for so many people?"

How were we to survive, then, in this new reality?

How were we to help others when we had no answers ourselves?

How were we to undo the pain of the past? What changes were we to make?

How were we to move forward when the future was uncertain at best?

How were we supposed to deal with all of this?

What were we supposed to do?

These questions and the thousands more that surfaced during that era—and in all truthfulness are filling the air still today—are legitimate ones. The times *are* uncertain. Life *does* feel fragile. When things are unsettled in the world at large, of course our souls take a hit. And yet to let fear run rampant in our feeble hearts is to sideline God for good. Fear is a prison. I don't say this as someone who never willingly walks into the cell and shuts the door behind me, but sadly as someone who does. We all do. Fear rises inside us all from time to time, and while we can't keep it at bay 100 percent of the time, we can absolutely keep it from making itself at home in our lives.

And well we should. Fear keeps us from enjoying life, siphoning joy from our spirits and leaving us leveled flat. Fear is unhelpful. Fear is unkind. Fear is unproductive, leading us down nothing but dead-end roads. "Fear never wrote a symphony or a poem," my friend Max Lucado wrote, "negotiated a peace treaty, or cured a disease. Fear never pulled a family out of poverty or a country out of bigotry. Fear never saved a marriage or a business. Courage did that. Faith did that. People who refuse to consult or cower to their timidities did that. But fear . . . herds us into a prison and slams the doors."[4]

When we give way to fear, we get in the way of the way of God. We tell him by our attitude and posture that we don't trust his will for us, his provision for us, his plans. We tell our good, good Father that he's not very good at all. If he were, wouldn't he have righted the wrong, relieved the suffering, solved the problem, settled the score? "Suffering does not obey our ultimatums,"[5] wrote author Jen Pollock Michel. Nor does God, as it turns out.

What he does do is promise to be with us (Isaiah 41:10), to help us (Isaiah 41:13), to have compassion on us (Isaiah 54:10), to give us wisdom (James 1:5), to meet our needs (Philippians 4:19), to give us strength when we're weary (Isaiah 40:29), to fight for us (Exodus 14:14), to ensure that no weapon forged against us will prevail (Isaiah 54:17), to secure our freedom (John 8:36), and to work together all things for good (Romans 8:28). And all along the way, he commits himself to this powerful claim that when we resist the devil, the devil will flee, as long as we're submitted to God.[6] No striving, no straining, no begging, no reaching, no boasting, no bragging, no showboating, no performing, no sulking, no moping, no regretting, no fretting—just unfettered focus on him.

Living Deceived

When we live *distracted*, we make our enemy's job immensely easier for him, which is also true when we allow ourselves to live *deceived*.

Satan's track record with deception is long-standing, stretching back to the garden of Eden when he smooth-talked Eve into believing that God's rules didn't apply to her. "Bread gained by deceit is sweet to a man, but afterward his mouth will be full of gravel," Proverbs 20:17 reminds us. Eve, and by extension, Adam, found this out the hard way when God expelled them from the land they loved.

Deception occurs whenever we surrender to the will and ways of Satan instead of the will and ways of God, and its effects run deep and long. "But You, O God, shall bring them down to the pit of destruction," Psalm 55:23 says; "bloodthirsty and deceitful men shall not live out half their days; but I will trust in You" (NKJV).

Scripture tells us that we can be deceived, such as was the case with Eve. And that we can be deceitful, such as was the case with Judas Iscariot, who betrayed Jesus in exchange for thirty silver coins. And that we can deceive ourselves, such as is the case with anyone who "thinks he is something, when he is nothing" (Galatians 6:3); who "thinks he is religious and does not bridle his tongue" (James 1:26); and who says he has no sin (see 1 John 1:8). But God's Word also tells us that the deceptive state is one we choose:

- "Do not be deceived," the apostle Paul exhorts us in 1 Corinthians 15:33. "'Bad company ruins good morals.'"
- "Let no one deceive you with empty words," he says to the church at Ephesus in Ephesians 5:6, "for because of these things [sexual immorality, impurity, covetousness, filthiness, foolish talk, crude joking, and idolatry] the wrath of God comes upon the sons of disobedience."
- "Let no one deceive you in any way," he tells the church at Thessalonica. "For that day [of Jesus' second coming and our being gathered together to him] will not come, unless the rebellion comes first, and the man of lawlessness is

revealed [meaning Satan], the son of destruction" (2 Thessalonians 2:3).

- "Little children, let no one deceive you," we read in 1 John 3:7. "Whoever practices righteousness is righteous, as he is righteous."

We can live free from deception. Doubt your doubts, and believe your beliefs. Exchange Satan's lies for God's truth. Trust God's Word, and reject the lies of the Enemy. Refuse to go deception's way.

Caving to Compromise

I'd like to address this third manner in which we play into Satan's hands—that of compromising on the standards God has asked us to uphold—by antithesis, by studying what it looks like to *refuse* to compromise.

In the Old Testament book of Exodus, we encounter Moses, a liberator, a law giver, and a leader like none the world had seen. This most revered prophet in Judaism had grown up in Egypt as the adopted son of Pharaoh, the king of Egypt, after his mother had cast him upon the waters of the Nile in a woven basket in hopes of sparing him from the law of the land requiring that all Hebrew baby boys be killed so that they wouldn't grow up to challenge Pharaoh's power.

In Exodus 3, Moses, a grown man living in Midian, keeping watch over his father-in-law's sheep, encountered a bush that was on fire but curiously was not being consumed. Moses stepped closer to investigate and heard a voice from heaven tell him to remove his shoes. He was on what God called "holy ground" (v. 5). God went on to tell Moses that he had a task for him to complete. God had heard the cries of his enslaved people in Egypt and wanted to use Moses to help set them free. Which was all well and good, except that Moses didn't like this plan. Moses was old—at least eighty years of age. He was tired. He was a stutterer. God wanted him to approach the king of Egypt and demand that God's people be freed?

Nah. Moses didn't think so. He'd rather keep tending sheep.

"I will be with you," God promised the prophet, "and this shall be the sign for you, that I have sent you: when you have brought the people out of Egypt, you shall serve God on this mountain" (v. 12).

What unfolded from there was a series of back-and-forth exchanges between Moses, Pharaoh, and God. Moses would demand the Israelites' freedom, to which Pharaoh would say no. Moses would tell God of Pharaoh's refusal, to which God would turn up the heat.

You'll recall that God's original mandate to Moses was to set the Israelites free. In Exodus 3:10, God said to Moses, "Come, I will send you to Pharaoh that you may bring my people, the children of Israel, out of Egypt."

Pretty clear, right?

When Pharaoh began to soften ever so slightly to the idea of releasing the Hebrew people from their bondage, he told Moses, in essence, "Fine, you can worship your God—whoever he is. But you must stay here, in this land."

At this point, Moses had two choices: He could compromise with God and accept Pharaoh's offer, or he could decide to stand firm.

He decided to stand firm.

Then came another three plagues—the first had been the city's water sources turning to blood, and that was followed by, of all things, frogs, gnats, and flies. And with these, another chance to compromise. "I'll let you go and worship your God," Pharaoh basically said, "as long as you don't go far."

You can be a Christian as long as you don't "go too far" with this thing—ever heard that advice? Don't "go too far" with that Bible reading. Don't "go too far" with that commitment to purity. Don't "go too far" with the priority of prayer. Don't "go too far" with sharing your faith. After all, you only live once. If you're going to enjoy life, now is the time! Don't let holiness steal all your fun.

You can take one foot out of Egypt, Pharaoh was telling Moses, as long as you keep one foot in. But is this what God was after? Moses knew the answer was no.

And so, plagues five, six, and seven—the death of the country's livestock, boils, and hail. At these, Pharaoh relented: "Plead with the LORD," he said to Moses in Exodus 9:28, "for there has been enough of God's thunder and hail. I will let you go, and you shall stay no longer." But this surrender was sadly short-lived. After Moses left the city and stretched out his hands to the Lord, God lifted the weight of the plagues, and Pharaoh was emboldened once more. "When Pharaoh saw that the rain and the hail and the thunder had ceased, he sinned yet again and hardened his heart, he and his servants. So the heart of Pharaoh was hardened, and he did not let the people of Israel go, just as the LORD had spoken through Moses" (Exodus 9:34–35).

Enter plagues eight, nine, and ten: locusts, darkness, death. And upon the angel of the Lord's passing over every Egyptian home, sparing the Hebrews and killing the firstborn sons of all others, Pharaoh at last let God's people go.

It would have been easy in the face of such overwhelming human power for Moses to compromise regarding what God had said. After all, surely God would understand that one man couldn't be expected to stand up to the king of the land time and time again, right? And yet Moses' example proves that when we are faithful to God's instructions, we bring freedom to those who are enslaved.

When I was a kid, the youth group I was part of used to sing a song at the end of worship services that said, "I have decided to follow Jesus. No turning back!" It was such a simple chorus, even as its sentiment is quite profound. Once you and I decide to follow Jesus, we ought to put a stake in the ground: no turning back.

No halfway faith.
No flip-flopping based on the times.
No wishy-washiness in us.
Never a compromise.

When Wisdom Has Its Way

The reason I have included this chapter on spiritual warfare here in our Part 1 discussion on the fundamentals of our faith is because there is a direct correlation between (a) our faithfulness to knowing and meditating on the Word of God, prioritizing prayer, and connecting with and leaning into a local church, and (b) our ability to render impotent Satan's schemes—and I trust you agree that we want those schemes rendered impotent in our lives! As we commit ourselves to learning and living out the holy Scriptures, keeping lines of communication open between God and us, and serving with joyful hearts in the context of his bride, the Church, we stay tethered to the fact that not only are we in a battle but also that *that battle's been won*. We are reminded that the battle is the Lord's, not ours. We are reminded that we aren't to set the bar at "survival" here on earth, but rather on *revival* throughout the land. We are reminded that because of Christ's great sacrifice, we live not for but *from* victory.

In the Old Testament book of Judges, we encounter the warrior Gideon, a hero of our faith. But when we meet him, he isn't aware that he's a warrior. "Hero" isn't exactly how he saw himself. An Israelite living under oppression in the land of Midian, Gideon was engaged in thankless, manual labor, beating out wheat in a winepress, when an angel of the Lord appeared. "The LORD is with you, O mighty man of valor," the angel said (Judges 6:12), to which Gideon essentially said, "Yeah, right."

Gideon had two issues with this angelic hello. First of all, if the Lord truly was "with" him, then why had he allowed his people, the Israelites, to suffer at the hand of the Midianites? Why hadn't they been rescued from being oppressed? Second, what kind of valiant man was relegated to beating out wheat in a winepress? Weren't their nobler things for the valiant to do?

Just as God had recruited Moses to save his people from slavery in Egypt, Gideon would be invited into a freedom fight. "I am calling you," God told him, "but I will be with you. You will not face the Midianites alone" (see Judges 6:16). Still, Gideon wasn't so sure. He was a nobody. He had nothing. He was weak. To which God offered reassurance that cut to the chase: "Peace be to you. Do not fear; you shall not die" (Judges 6:23).

The Midianite army numbered nearly half a million fighters, which was top-of-mind for Gideon now; at last count he had 32,000, all of whom were untrained volunteers. Which is probably why his jaw dropped when God told him his army was too big.

"Come again?"

"Yep. Too big. Whittle to just those who are unafraid."

Well, that took care of 22,000 of Gideon's 32,000 men, leaving him with just 10,000 now. He took a deep breath, steadied his stance, and with a sigh said, "We can do this," as God inhaled to speak again. "Still too many, Gideon. Three hundred men—no more."

Three hundred against half a *million*?

This was beyond absurd. And yet Gideon trusted God. And God, true to form, showed up. Judges 6:33–34 reports that as the opposing armies were lining up to take down Gideon's men, all the "Midianites and the Amalekites and the people of the East," the "Spirit of the Lord clothed Gideon." If that image doesn't put a hitch in your throat, maybe *your* heart has hardened some.

When Gideon had reached a breaking point, God said, "I will wrap myself around you, so that you *know* that I am near." God wanted Gideon to wear him like a suit. He wanted to be so close to Gideon that when Gideon made a move, God made that same move. Such presence. Such covering. Such *grace*. It was just what Gideon needed.

The story of Gideon's victory is so good that it is worth your time to read Judges 6–8 on your own. In the end, that paltry assembly of three hundred men not only handily defeated the opposition, but because of his great leadership, the people of Israel begged Gideon to be their king. "I will not rule over you," Gideon said by way of reply, "and my son will not rule over you" (Judges 8:23). Guess who would rule over them? *The Lord*. Which brings me to our three truths about warfare, for believers of every stripe: The battle is the Lord's. We're not meant merely to survive but to thrive, to lead *revival* throughout the land. And we fight not for victory but from it, for the war has already been won.

When we say yes to God, and yes to his Word, and yes to communion with him, and yes to fellowship with his saints, we in essence clothe ourselves with divine power and protection from whatever Satan has up his sleeve. Yes, we soberly remember that we are in a battle. But we also remember that victory is ours.

PART TWO

Swaps That
Support Reignition

5

Exchanging Doubt for Faith

Faith expects from God what is beyond all expectation.

Andrew Murray,
In Search of God's Perfection

Count it all joy, my brothers, when you meet trials of various kinds, for you know that the testing of your faith produces steadfastness. And let steadfastness have its full effect, that you may be perfect and complete, lacking in nothing. . . . Blessed is the man who remains steadfast under trial, for when he has stood the test he will receive the crown of life, which God has promised to those who love him.

James 1:2–4, 12

In Part 1, we looked at four pillars of the Christian faith—reading and applying God's Word; prioritizing the practice of prayer; engaging meaningfully in the body of Christ, the Church; and living each day from the victory that God has secured for us through Jesus Christ. And while it's true that building a life on these pillars will provide a firm foundation on which to stand, it's also true that the forces of this world will do everything in their power to jostle us and shake us and knock us clean off that steady place. Despite our fervent efforts, we won't always stand perfectly firm.

In the apostle Paul's letter to the believers gathered in Ephesus, he encouraged them to prize "unity of the faith and of the knowledge of the Son of God" so that they would "no longer be children, tossed to and fro by the waves and carried about by every wind of doctrine, by human cunning, by craftiness in deceitful schemes" (Ephesians 4:13–14). As we mature in Christ, that "tossing about" is admittedly minimized, but oh, how much damage can be done along the way. It's maddening as faithful believers living in an undoubtedly broken world that we keep getting slammed into the water's depth and left with a throat full of salt water while desperately gasping for breath. Where is the predictability we long for? Where is the security we seek?

We want *financial* security. I've seen more than my fair share of economic downturns and have therefore walked with countless people through the arduous process of picking up the pieces and moving ahead on the heels of job losses, market plunges, restructurings, reorganizations, and the decimation of their 401(k) accounts. Especially tragic was the hit we collectively took in 2008 and 2009 when *half the world's wealth* disappeared.[1] I remember talking with friends one day, shaking my head over a *Forbes* retrospective I'd seen, which said that during this two-year period, the number of billionaires fell by a full 30 percent.[2] "Poor, pitiful them!" my friends said with a laugh. And yet when such global wealth falls down, it takes the rest of us with it! As I write this, the latest hit we've suffered—economic fallout due to the pandemic—is still punching us in the face, and if trends hold, one in three will be unemployed when this thing finally peters out.[3]

We also want *physical* security. I'm part of the population that is often heard bemoaning unforeseen health challenges, inadequate health coverage, and an uncertain future regarding our ability to participate fully in life. Chronic-pain sufferers wonder if relief will ever be in sight. Moms and dads of kids with special needs wonder if they'll ever feel rested again. Adult children wonder how they're supposed to balance the needs of their own families with the ever-increasing needs of aging parents. People with diseased bodies or mental-health challenges or disabilities of any kind wonder why they drew the short straw.

For far too many people, the longing for *food* security is all too real. Today, more than 11 percent of Americans report not having adequate nutrition day by day.[4] On a global scale, the regular caloric intake of 11 percent of men, women, and children is far less than the energy they expend. This equates to 820 *million* people who simply don't have enough food to eat.[5]

We want *national and international* security, desperate for terrorist activities to be curtailed, hopeful for peace in the Middle East and also in our streets.

We want *relational* security, eager for marriages to thrive, for family members to engage, and for friendships to stand the test of time.

We want *emotional* security, for the fog to lift that we find ourselves feeling our way through from time to time, for the flows to outnumber the ebbs for once, for the darkness to brighten a bit. Famed author J. K. Rowling, who has been quite candid about her own battle with depression, described it as the "cold absence of feeling," as being "hollowed-out."[6]

I can relate to those sentiments. Depression left me feeling like a fragile shell of myself.

Well, we know from God's Word that security is found only when we dwell "in the shelter of the Most High" (Psalm 91:1), but how do we get to that place of supernatural steadiness? How is that firm footing found?

If you've ever ordered an article of clothing online and received it in the mail, only to realize upon putting the thing on that it doesn't fit you right, then you know how satisfying it is to have a customer-service representative tell you, "No problem whatsoever. Let's get you something that fits you. Oh, and by the way, no charge."

It's refreshing, isn't it, to be rid of the ill-fitting garment and in possession of one that works? It is no stretch to say that our heavenly Father works just like that rep. God knows that in this sin-scarred life on this sin-scarred planet, you and I will face difficult things. We will see ugliness, we will feel anguished, we will have questions, we will know pain. But here is the amazing part: When we are faithful to take those awful, agonizing exposures and experiences to him, he is faithful to replace them with the redeemed, the glorious, the good. "I will bring 'good news to the poor,'" God promises his people through his prophet Isaiah (see Isaiah 61:1). And what person suffering the chronic bad news of poverty wouldn't sign up for an exchange like that?

Further, in the same passage of Scripture (see vv. 1–3), God offers his people healing in exchange for brokenheartedness, freedom in exchange for captivity, comfort in exchange for grief, gladness in exchange for mourning, praise in exchange for faith that has grown feeble, and a sturdy and righteous reputation in exchange for the faintness we all feel from time to time.

There are perhaps *hundreds* of divine exchanges we could choose to dissect together, and we'd no doubt benefit tremendously from the exercise. But given my publisher's insistence that you have other things to do than to read a thousand-page book, I've limited myself to three. Because the three exchanges that we'll scrutinize in this part—exchanging doubt for faith, exchanging discontentment for gratitude, and exchanging disordered thinking for peace—rise to the surface of reignition's relevance more than any others I could choose, I believe they will be of greatest benefit to you. First up: laying down doubt and picking up faith.

Faith *always* fits just right.

We Sink, Jesus Soothes

Had you and I been there that day, I'm sure we'd have rubbed our eyes in disbelief. Jesus had left the crowds that always surrounded him to ascend a mountain, alone, and pray. He'd sent his disciples across the sea ahead of him, telling them he'd meet them on the other side. But the weather had a different plan in mind that night, one involving tumultuous wind and waves. Matthew recorded that the disciples' boat was in the middle of the sea, being tossed by the waves and, in his words, a "contrary" wind (Matthew 14:24 NKJV). It was the fourth watch of the night when Jesus came walking on the sea, and "when the disciples saw Him walking on the sea," verse 26 reads, "they were troubled" (NKJV).

Saying the disciples were "troubled" here is like saying I feel "bummed" every year when my beloved Dallas Cowboys fail to take the top spot again. Those men were absolutely, positively *freaked out*. The fourth watch of the night would have been just before daybreak, when the sky is as dark as it ever will be, and to have what appeared to be a ghost closing in on them during a terrifying storm would have left even the strongest constitution undone. They "cried out in fear," the text tells us (v. 26), to which this "ghost" immediately replied, "Be of good cheer! It is I; do not be afraid" (v. 27 NKJV).

Given the circumstances surrounding the disciples, I absolutely love that line. *Be of good cheer*, Jesus? Here? Now?

Peter was the one to speak first: "Lord, if it is You," he said, "command me to come to You on the water," to which Jesus looked his way and said, "Come" (vv. 28–29 NKJV).

Peter climbed out of the boat, the text says, and he walked. On the water. Toward his Lord. All went well . . . for a few seconds, anyway. "But when he saw that the wind was boisterous," verse 30 says, "he was afraid; and beginning to sink he cried out, saying, 'Lord, save me!'" (NKJV).

As one does, right?

This next part is what I want to draw your attention to. When Jesus noticed that Peter was sinking, he did something remarkable. Verse 31 says that he "immediately . . . stretched out His hand and caught him." He then asked Peter why his faith had failed him: "O you of little faith, why did you doubt?" (v. 31 NKJV). And in that moment of reckoning, the wind, according to verse 32, ceased.

Be of good cheer!

It is I; be not afraid.

O you of little faith . . .

Why on earth did you doubt?

Jesus reaches down and with a heart of compassion stills both the internal storm of doubt in Peter and the external storm threatening his world. He longs to do the same thing in and for us.

Jesus Watches Us

If I were to ask you to draw a picture of Jesus and Peter during that incredible walking-on-water scene, which direction would Jesus be facing? Would he be facing Peter or looking away? My guess is that ten out of ten people would portray Jesus with his gaze *immovably fixed* on his disciple as that young man stutter-stepped his way atop the waves. How could he *not* watch Peter trying to navigate the liquid terrain? On so many occasions, sufferers of this thing called life ask me, as a pastor, "Where was God?"

Where was God when my kid ran away?

Where was God when my wife was in the car accident?

Where was God when my boss misrepresented me and caused me to lose my job?

Where was God when my family could barely make ends meet all those months?

Where was God when the bottom was falling out?

Where was God when you were struggling with whatever you were last struggling with?

Where was God when I was wrestling with depression?

Where was God, you ask? Right there, watching you. Watching me. Watching every person who ever has suffered any misfortune. "The eyes of the LORD are in every place," Proverbs 15:3 promises, "watching the evil and the good" (NASB). Which means that while you and I may temporarily lose sight of Jesus, he never loses sight of us. He "always lives to make intercession" for us, Hebrews 7:25 says . . . our Savior, ever ready to help.

Think of it: Regardless of the storm you're presently facing, there is Jesus, eyes fixed on you, lips moving in prayer to the Father on your behalf.

He sees.

He knows.

He cares.

He is near.

He is here.

And he is eager to intervene.

Jesus Comes to Us

Not only does Jesus *see* us when we're struggling but he also *comes to us*. Remember, the account involving Peter occurred during the darkest hour of the night. And here, at the bleakest point, is when Jesus showed up. I think about that scene from time to time when my circumstances taunt me. "You're always on time," I tell God, as though he doesn't already know that to be true. Have you ever thought about that? God is never early. He is never late. He is always on time. His intervention is always perfectly timed. "For those whom he foreknew he also predestined to be conformed to the image of his Son," says Romans 8:29, "in order that he might be the firstborn among many brothers." Those circumstances that we begrudge are the very tools in the hands of the Master that chip away what doesn't belong as we become more and more like Christ. Those financial storms and relational storms and emotional storms and health-related storms we beg God to take away? Each storm is serving the purpose of making us more like him.

Even so, at the right moment, when we are just *sure* we're going under, Jesus shows up to remind us that the very situations that assail us remain utterly under his feet. The misfortune is under his feet. The job loss is under his feet. The fear is under his feet. The hunger is under his feet. The affair is under his feet. The addiction is under his feet. The abuse is under his feet. *Everything that threatens us* is under the feet of Jesus, whom God chose to make right the brokenness of this fallen world by humbly facing death on a cross. Which is why I can tell you with 100 percent certainty that this Christ is worthy of our steadfast faith.

Faith, and Why It Matters

In perhaps the best-known verse on the subject, Hebrews 11:1 tells us that "faith is the assurance of things hoped for, the conviction [or the evidence] of things not seen." And the reason we ought to care deeply about what it means to understand faith and possess faith and live by faith is because a few verses later, in Hebrews 11:6, we learn that *without* faith, it is impossible to please God. I once heard a pastor say that if you please God, it doesn't matter whom you displease. But if you displease God, it doesn't matter whom you please, and I find these words to ring true. Adrian Rogers once said, quoting Jesus' response in Matthew 9:29 to the two blind men whom Jesus had healed, "According to your faith be it done to you. Not according to your fame, or according to your finances, or according to your fortune, or according to your fate, but according to your *faith* be it done to you. It is only by faith that we may please God."

My preacher friends and I called those little minisermons "Adrianisms." How I miss him.

From that reminder we see that, as believers, we're not merely to be *saved* by faith, which is obviously a critical step, but also to *live* by faith. We are "saved by grace through faith," Paul says in Ephesians 2:8 (CSB), and also, "the just shall live by faith" (Hebrews 10:38 NKJV). We are saved by faith; we are to live by faith; we are *saved to live* by faith.

I want to camp out here for a few moments, because if you and I can grasp this idea that we are saved to live by faith, then we will be able to make the first of the three exchanges we are talking about here, that of exchanging doubt for faith. Whenever we encounter a trial in life, instead of sinking under the weight of our fearsome situation, we will remember that God has promised to bless and keep those who look to him. The fact is, we all are summoned to a test in life. You'll be having a beautiful day in the sunshine when out of the clear blue your cellphone rings. It's the call you didn't want to receive: the diagnosis, the dismissal, the news. It's wild turbulence during the darkest hour of the night—the wind, the waves, the storm. And yes, while we can whimper and whine and cry out for help, we have another course available to us. We can do what the apostle James said to do: We can start counting our trials as *joy*.

Upside of the Struggle

The fact is, as counterintuitive as it seems, we are to *celebrate* when we share in the sufferings of Jesus, because we know that we are influencing the world for him. "Whatever gain I had, I counted as loss for the sake of Christ," wrote the apostle Paul in Philippians 3. "Indeed, I count everything as loss because of the surpassing worth of knowing Christ Jesus my Lord. For his sake I have suffered the loss of all things and count them as rubbish, in order that I may gain Christ and be found in him, not having a righteousness of my own that comes from the law, but that which comes through faith in Christ, the righteousness from God that depends on faith—that I may know him and the power of his resurrection, and may share his sufferings, becoming like him in his death, that by any means possible I may attain the resurrection from the dead" (vv. 7–11).

Struggles build in us a righteousness that depends not on our own strength or savvy, but rather "on faith," to quote Paul. In other words, the manner in which we face and overcome challenges in our lives can *point the watching world toward faith in Jesus Christ*. But as I say, we won't view trials and tribulations this way unless we intend to; this exchange of doubt for faith requires *meaningful work* on our part. And where does this work begin? With remembering the divine purposes of trials. What good are our struggles, anyway? Let's look at the upside that unfolds every time.

Our Faith Is Confirmed

For many believers I've met, their salvation story involves their bottoming out before accepting God's gift of grace. In fact, most people I know at some point in their lives believed that they would make a pretty good god. And so they ran their lives on their own, creating all their own rules, making all their own decisions, doing exactly as they pleased. This approach worked well, they will tell you, until the day it didn't. And on that day, a spectacular fall ensued as the self-made empire they'd erected came crashing down at their feet. Which is perhaps why our heavenly Father has to apply some degree of diligence to finding people who will let him be God. "For the eyes of the LORD run to and fro throughout the whole earth," 2 Chronicles 16:9 says, "to give strong support to those whose heart is blameless toward him."

God is searching our homes, our neighborhoods, our businesses, our eating establishments, our politicians' offices, our churches, our factories, our schools, our hospitals, our grocery stores, our homeless shelters, our gyms, our nursing homes, everywhere . . . looking for someone—*anyone*—whom he might bless. He is scanning in search of faithful followers of his, the person who in the face of difficult circumstances will not waver but will trust in him. "The crucible is for silver and the furnace for gold," wrote Solomon in Proverbs 27:21 (NASB). Oh, that we would view our challenges as staging areas for splendor, as preambles to prevailing in Christ. That we would say with Job the tormented, "Naked I came from my mother's womb, and naked shall I return. The LORD gave, and the LORD has taken away; blessed be the name of the LORD. . . . Though he slay me, I will hope in him. . . . When he has tried me, I shall come out as gold" (Job 1:21; 13:15; 23:10).

Whenever we wrestle with unwelcome circumstances, we can take heart that God is at work. He is scanning the horizon, eager to come to us with aid, faithful Father to the child in need who is sinking fast beneath the waves.

Our Stance Is Stabilized

A second purpose of trials connects directly with the first, which is that our stance is stabilized. Think of it: If it's true that we seek God more often when we are facing turbulence than when we are sailing along on serene seas, then during and after trials and tribulation is when we receive an infusion of his compassion and care. That infusion ministers deeply to us by shoring us up and steadying our stance. "I waited patiently for the LORD," David wrote in Psalm 40; "he inclined to me and heard my cry. He drew me up from the pit of destruction, out of the miry bog, and set my feet upon a rock, making my steps secure" (vv. 1–2).

When we encounter hardship and are tempted to doubt the goodness of God, we can instead reaffirm our belief that that challenge is God's *stabilizing service* in our lives. "I know that I will emerge from this difficulty steadier than I was before," we can tell him. "I know that even as the ground beneath me feels shaky like shifting sand, your power is sure, your ways are reliable, and you will plant me on solid ground."

Our Minds Are Matured

It has been said that learning arrives in four layers, knowledge of a thing being merely level one; anyone can master a series of facts, and in that regard he or she can "know" the material. The next layer is belief: We apprehend the sequence of winter following autumn following summer following spring, and then, based on empirical evidence year after year, we believe that the sequence is so. This is, by the way, where most churches cease their discipleship efforts: "Here! Take all this information about God, about Jesus, about the Holy Spirit, about sin, about forgiveness, about grace . . . and then believe it to be true."

They clap the dust off their hands and call it a day, as if to say that their work here is done. But have the disciples actually been discipled? Have they *learned* anything at all?

Level three is conviction. We hold beliefs; convictions hold us. People don't die for beliefs but for convictions. Convictions make us go all in.

And then there's level four, which is application. "Don't be hearers of the word only," James essentially says, "but doers of the word" (see James 1:22).

Whenever I get asked about long-range goals for Prestonwood, where I pastor, my answer is always the same: Over the next ten, twenty, however many years I am honored to lead the church, my singular goal is that every member of our congregation would come to a place of spiritual maturity that is marked not only by their knowing God or believing God but also by the reality of God defining their convictions, by the ways of God laying the rails on which their lives run. I'm told that the late Dallas Theological Seminary professor and brilliant scholar Howard Hendricks once likened too many Christians to "a bad photograph: overexposed and underdeveloped." Using that verbiage, my goal for believers in my care is that they'd be fully developed in Christ. And if we are to believe the Bible, then we understand that such development comes only by way of turmoil, of trials, of tests. When I was a little boy, my legs would sometimes ache, and my mother would massage them until they settled down again. "Jackie, these are just growing pains," she would say, her voice as soothing as her touch. Pain produces growth—that's the message she conveyed. Spiritually speaking, this is also true: It is through suffering and surviving life's myriad challenges that we carve out the character we need.

Think of the Old Testament's King David, whose path was far from straight. Yes, he would indeed slay a giant, write beautiful songs and poetry, worship God with unrivaled devotion, and serve honorably as Israel's king. But his journey would also include some pretty spectacular stumbles—namely an adulterous affair, the carrying out of a murderous plot, a deceptive cover-up, the unnecessary death of his son. And yet we gather from David's experience that regardless of the ill-advised tangents we may take in our lives, when we allow God to cement our beliefs as conviction and channel that conviction into demonstrable acts, the rash curvatures need not define us; faithful people will be known for their faith.

When I was a kid, I couldn't get enough of the seminal story of David's life, his takedown of a trash-talking thug. I would beg every believing adult in my life to "tell me again" of the nine-footer, of the smooth stones, of the fearlessness on display. I especially remember sitting on my grandfather's lap as he read the Scriptures to me, and after I'd indulged his methodical meanderings through the Psalms, the Gospels, the Epistles, I'd flip pages until we landed in 1 Samuel. "Let's do David and Goliath again!" I'd cheer. David was a man after God's own heart, 1 Samuel 13:14 says. He was a man after my own heart too.

Let me refresh the context, in case it's been a while since you've revisited the familiar story.

A group of Hebrew farmers had formed an army and had vanquished their archenemy, the Philistines. The defeated group, now enraged, was on the prowl for vengeance, determined to put the Israelites in their place. As the Philistines collected on one side of a valley, and the Israelites on the other, the battle lines were drawn.

As Israel's army strategized on how to finish off the victory they'd already once gained, they heard the thunderous sound of footsteps as though the earth were giving way. They heard him before they saw him, profanity and blasphemy filling the valley's expanse. The killing machine's name was Goliath; his armor alone weighed two hundred pounds.

"Send the best fighter you've got!" Goliath jeered. "Whoever wins takes the other side captive." For forty days, this was the bet.

I reread this account during those long days of depression and could nearly smell Goliath's breath as he issued this heartless threat. The giants we face taunt us just as mercilessly, don't they? Giants of stress. Giants of discouragement. Giants of fear. They stand there yelling at us daily, "Come on, loser! Why won't you fight?"

Their sheer size makes us feel miniscule, insignificant, ridiculous, and weak, which is exactly how the nation of Israel was feeling the day young David happened onto the scene.

Ironically, David showed up not as a soldier, but rather as the equivalent of a pizza-delivery boy bringing sustenance to the fighting men. King Saul had forfeited his throne because of his misbehavior, and David had been anointed the new king. But it would be several decades before he'd assume his position; for now, he was just a boy. But that boy would become a man the day he heard a giant mocking his God.

"What's going on here?" David asked, incredulous. "Why isn't anyone shutting him up?"

"David," the boy's brothers said, motioning toward Goliath, "don't you see how huge he is?" to which David said, "Don't you know how big *God* is?"

"He's too big to hit!" the brothers counseled.

"He's too big to *miss*," David replied.

And so the plan was set. After requesting and receiving permission from Saul to engage Goliath, David grabbed his slingshot and marched off toward the beast. In the late Eugene Peterson's poetic retelling of 1 Samuel 17, we read what happened next:

Then David took his shepherd's staff, selected five smooth stones from the brook, and put them in the pocket of his shepherd's pack, and with his sling in his hand approached Goliath.

As the Philistine paced back and forth, his shield bearer in front of him, he noticed David. He took one look down on him and sneered—a mere youngster, apple-cheeked and peach-fuzzed.

The Philistine ridiculed David. "Am I a dog that you come after me with a stick?" And he cursed him by his gods.

"Come on," said the Philistine. "I'll make roadkill of you for the buzzards. I'll turn you into a tasty morsel for the field mice."

David answered, "You come at me with sword and spear and battle-ax. I come at you in the name of GOD-of-the-Angel-Armies, the God of Israel's troops, whom you curse and mock. This very day GOD is handing you over to me. I'm about to kill you, cut off your head, and serve up your body and the bodies of your Philistine buddies to the crows and coyotes. The whole earth will know that there's an extraordinary God in Israel. And everyone gathered here will learn that GOD doesn't save by means of sword or spear. The battle belongs to GOD—he's handing you to us on a platter!"

That roused the Philistine, and he started toward David. David took off from the front line, running toward the Philistine. David reached into his pocket for a stone, slung it, and hit the Philistine hard in the forehead, embedding the stone deeply. The Philistine crashed, facedown in the dirt.

That's how David beat the Philistine—with a sling and a stone. He hit him and killed him. No sword for David!

Then David ran up to the Philistine and stood over him, pulled the giant's sword from its sheath, and finished the job by cutting off his head. When the Philistines saw that their great champion was dead, they scattered, running for their lives.

The men of Israel and Judah were up on their feet, shouting! They chased the Philistines all the way to the outskirts of Gath and the gates of Ekron. Wounded Philistines were strewn along the Shaaraim road all the way to Gath and Ekron. After chasing the Philistines, the Israelites came back and looted their camp. David took the Philistine's head and brought it to Jerusalem. But the giant's weapons he placed in his own tent.

vv. 40–54 MSG

It is when we rise to life's challenges that our faith is confirmed, our stance is stabilized, and our minds are matured. It is when we face down our giants that the whole earth knows there's an extraordinary God in our neck of the woods who saves by neither sword nor spear.

Because of this reality, like young David, we can choose not to cower in the face of adversity, but rather to run *toward* the beasts that threaten us So, run! Not in fear but in courage in the face of your biggest challenges. Never be diminished by giants that make you feel small.

The Choice for Faith

To follow Jesus is to come frequently to a figurative fork in the road where we must choose between faith and doubt. The two can't be pursued simultaneously: To opt for faith is to let go of doubt, if even momentarily, in the same way that going means stopping has ceased. At this fork, I find that when I engage in two specific practices, they help me to choose wisely. First, I remember God's faithfulness. Second, I renew my commitment to him.

Remember God's Faithfulness to You

In his spectacular book *The Practice of Godliness*, author Jerry Bridges asks us to consider afresh the "absolute necessity of the faithfulness of God."[7] He writes: "We are dependent upon his faithfulness for our final salvation (see 1 Corinthians 1:8–9), for deliverance from temptation (see 1 Corinthians 10:13), for ultimate sanctification (see 1 Thessalonians 5:23), for the forgiveness of our sins (see 1 John 1:9), for deliverance through times of suffering (see 1 Peter 4:19), and for the fulfillment of our ultimate hope of eternal life (see Hebrews 10:23). We can easily see that every aspect of the Christian life rests upon the faithfulness of God."[8] Such faithfulness the Father has demonstrated toward us time and again, and yet how quickly we tend to forget these things he's done for us! And so we must willfully and with determination *remember*.

Renew Your Faith in Him

The choice for faith is simply choosing to remember—that God is good, that God is near, that God is committed to save and serve and heal. And because he is committed to us, we can be confident in committing to him. Which brings us to that second practice I mentioned: actively placing our trust in him.

When I was a boy growing up in a modest home on the east side of Fort Worth, Texas, I thumbtacked a bookmark to the little bulletin board my mom had hung on my bedroom wall that boasted a now-famous painting of Jesus standing behind the captain of a sailing vessel who was positioned at the helm. The captain's hand was on the ship's steering wheel, and Jesus' hand was on the shoulder of the captain. Not long ago, a few of my colleagues and I were in Fort Worth for a meeting, and I asked if they'd indulge me for a few minutes while I drove by that childhood home. They said, "Sure," and were being good sports about it, until I parked the car in front of that house and began to climb out. "You're going *in*?" they said.

I figured it never hurts to ask.

The owner of the house I grew up in looked more than a little perplexed to find a guy in a suit and tie knocking on his door, but after I offered a brief explanation, he let me in. And as I stood in that tiny back-hall bedroom, a flood of emotion washed over me. I walked over to the wall where that bulletin board used to hang and thought about the words of Proverbs 3:5–6, which accompanied the picture of the captain at sea: "Trust in the LORD with all your heart, and do not lean on your own understanding. In all your ways acknowledge him, and he will make straight your paths."

With my palm flat against my old bedroom wall, I recounted God's faithfulness to that promise across all the years I'd lived since I occupied that space. I thought about how fervently I'd tried to trust him, how diligently I'd tried to go his way instead of mine, how passionately I'd tried to acknowledge him, how *faithful* I hoped I'd been. And then and there, I resolved all over again to believe his promise that my future was utterly secure. "[God] is able to do far more abundantly than all that we ask or think, according to the power at work within us," we always say around Prestonwood, quoting Paul's letter to the followers of Jesus gathered in Ephesus, recorded in Ephesians 3:20–21.

By faith we believe those words to be true.

By faith we live as though those words are true.

6

Exchanging Discontentment for Gratitude

The LORD is my shepherd; I shall not want.
He makes me lie down in green pastures.
He leads me beside still waters.
He restores my soul.
He leads me in paths of righteousness
for his name's sake.
Even though I walk through the valley of the shadow
of death,
I will fear no evil,
for you are with me;
your rod and your staff,
they comfort me.
You prepare a table before me
in the presence of my enemies;
you anoint my head with oil;
my cup overflows.
Surely goodness and mercy shall follow me
all the days of my life,
and I shall dwell in the house of the LORD forever.

Psalm 23

It's said of some that as they get *older*, they get *colder*. Perhaps you've noticed, as I have, that as some folks get up there in years, they become a little grumpy, a little cynical, a little difficult to please. The fact is, the longer a person lives here in this broken world, the easier it is to gripe. Twenty-somethings are generally pretty optimistic about the future and their role in shaping it; teens believe themselves to be utterly impervious to the goings-on in the world around them, and children are impossibly cheerful—life is a *playground* for them. But for those in their thirties, forties, fifties, and beyond? Stuff *bugs* us, and increasingly we want to talk about it. We're a gripe-fest in search of an ear.

"Thirty?" you ask. "Thirty is *old*?" It's well on its way, I'm afraid. "When your body's metabolism starts slowing in your 30s, so, too, does the bioenergy of skin cells, which powers the creation of collagen, activates repair processes," writes journalist Grace Gold. Dr. Alexa Kimball, professor of dermatology at Harvard Medical School, says, "When bioenergy drops, it's like your skin is getting tired and no longer firing on all cylinders."[1] Yeah. Which of us can't say amen to that? And it's not just our skin that sags—am I right? Our bodies and brains sag too.

Need proof? If you're over the age of thirty, you can probably name twenty things that bug you now that never bugged you before.

These days, older adults find plenty to complain about. They gripe about politics. Or about the weather. Or about the traffic. Or about potholes. They gripe about the server getting their lunch order wrong. Or about the person in front of them at the grocery store having thirteen items in a lane marked out for twelve. And then there's their health. Heavens, their blessed health. Their kidneys aren't working right. They have to have their spleen taken out. Their stomach is always upset. They have the bladder of an infant again. I call this litany the "organ recital." I hear a performance most every day.

You know from the last chapter of my affinity for King David, and I'd like to lean into his legacy once more as we dissect the second of three exchanges I promised you we could make. At any point, on any occasion, you and I can trade our doubt for faith. What a powerful weapon of warfare this is, given the faithless days in which we live! But equally powerful is this: We can trade *discontentment for gratitude*. We don't have to get colder as we get older; we can live willfully thankful lives.

David is one of only seven known contributors to the book of Psalms and is thought to have penned between 73 and 85 of the 150 entries we know and love. (In case curiosity is getting the better of you, Asaph and the three sons of Korah are the other major writers; Solomon, Moses, Ethan, and Heman are the minor writers; and a full 50 of the psalms are unattributed, believed to have been passed down through oral tradition rather than hailing from a singular source.) But of all the psalms David wrote, his most beloved one is surely Psalm 23.

Scholars aren't able to place the writing of Psalm 23 at a specific time in David's life, because there are no solid details offered in its words that might point to a given year. Still, everyone agrees that he wrote it later in life, significant experience now under his belt. Given that timing, David could have found fault with life, a man on his way to being old, and thus cold. The Amalekites were harassing him. The Edomites wouldn't leave him alone. The Syrians were threatening destruction. The Jebusites were angry again.

And then there was the fallout from the Bathsheba disaster.

The census that had gone awry.

The son who had proved rebellious and one greedy as the day was long.

The incessant challenges of leading a people for forty full years.

David could have complained and whined and become a miserable old man.

But guess what David did instead? He wrote Psalm 23.

Reasons to Give Thanks

The Twenty-third Psalm has been called the greatest poem penned in any language, and to read it aloud is to hear that poetry—the cadence, the lyric, the serene and sweet-spoken song. Just this week, as I sought to comfort a couple wading through deep waters, I quoted its words, and true to form, the peace that flooded our conversation was sure. "The LORD is my shepherd," David begins; "I shall not want" (v. 1). And then he goes on to enumerate the ways that his heavenly Father provides for his needs.

To meditate on David's sentiments is to see why scholars time this writing later in his life. Why would a soul need restoring unless it had been battered by life's swift winds? What adolescent or twentysomething concerns himself much with the "valley of the shadow of death"? How many enemies does a child truly know? No, here we have the ponderings of an experienced man, one who has been on the path for quite some time, one who has gained—or is gaining, at least—perspective on the journey of life.

"Thank you for your presence . . ."

The first verse of Psalm 23 confirms that the Lord "is" David's shepherd—and thus also ours. He didn't say that the Lord *used to be* his shepherd, or that maybe someday the Lord *would be* his shepherd, but rather that today, this day—here and now—God was leading him as a shepherd would.

When the great Old Testament Moses encountered God in a burning bush and was divinely tasked with delivering the children of Israel from enslavement, God told the man that his name was "I AM" (see Exodus 3:14). The original Hebrew word there points to existence, to being, to life. God's referring to himself as I Am was his way of naming his self-existence, his eternality, his presence outside the boundaries of time. "In the beginning, God . . ." Moses wrote in Genesis 1:1, which is quite a confounding statement to ponder. Before all else was here, God was here? How do our brains explain *that*?

The great preacher Shadrach Meshach Lockridge once spoke on this psalm, using only those first three words as his source text: "The Lord is . . ." And despite the dubious grammar, my favorite section from the entire sermon is when Pastor S. M. said, "The Lord *is*! The Lord *always has been* is! And the Lord *always will be* is!"

I say amen to that! "Jesus Christ is the same yesterday, today, and forever," the writer of Hebrews said in chapter 13, verse 8 (NLT), which means that God's greatness and glory have forever been and forever will be glorious and great. Isn't that refreshing to consider? Unlike you and I, who break down a little bit with each year that passes and wonder why we can't do all that we used to do, God's goodness and his greatness and his prowess and his power will never be diminished or compromised.

God, who is kind, will *always* be kind.

God, who is compassionate, will *always* be compassionate.

God, who is wise, will *always* be wise.

"The LORD is my shepherd," David wrote, acknowledging that God, who is present, will *always* be here.

"Thank you for your personal touch . . ."

It is said that the great reformer Martin Luther stated that the heart of Christianity is seen in its personal pronouns, and in that first line, we feel the effect: "The LORD is *my* shepherd," David wrote . . . not "a" shepherd but *mine*. The Good Shepherd knows his sheep by name (see John 10:14), and based on the myriad trips to the Middle East I've enjoyed, it would be notable if God did *not*.

In the same way that people in the United States name and often humanize their pets—dogs and cats and birds and all the rest—shepherds in the Middle East name and humanize their sheep. They don't merely tolerate their sheep; they adore their sheep . . . in the same way that God adores us. "He will tend his flock like a shepherd," the prophet Isaiah says. "He will gather the lambs in his arms; he will carry them in his bosom, and gently lead those that are with young" (Isaiah 40:11). That image has comforted me on more days than I can count—the image of being gathered up by my good Father and tucked into his chest, safe from the storms that loom overhead, from the devastation that comes to us daily, threatening to do us in. He joyfully carries us—do you realize that? After *eagerly* coming to us.

In Luke 15, we find poignant proof of the Good Shepherd's affection for his sheep. "Now the tax collectors and sinners were all drawing near to hear him," the story begins, referring to Jesus. "And the Pharisees and the scribes grumbled, saying, 'This man receives sinners and eats with them.'

"So he told them this parable: 'What man of you, having a hundred sheep, if he has lost one of them, does not leave the ninety-nine in the open country, and go after the one that is lost, until he finds it? And when he has found it, he lays it on his shoulders, rejoicing. And when he comes home, he calls together his friends and his neighbors, saying to them, 'Rejoice with me, for I have found my sheep that was lost.' Just so, I tell you, there will be more joy in heaven over one sinner who repents than over ninety-nine righteous persons who need no repentance" (vv. 1–7).

One person warrants this attention from God! *One.*

Our followership is personal to him.

"Thank you for being proactive . . ."

In characterizing sheep behavior, it would be fair to say that they are a wandering mob. They stick together, but if you convince the lead sheep to step right off a cliff in search of greener grass down below, irrationally the rest of the herd will follow. Which is perhaps why no school worth its endowment picks as its mascot the sheep. With the Boll Weevils, the Wampus Cats, the Sand Gnats (I'm not making this up), the Jackrabbits, and the Mud Hens, there are some questionable mascots out there. But still, I defy you to find the Sheep. *Nobody* picks the sheep.

Nobody wants to be associated with an animal known not for leading but for following, and yet when it comes to how God hopes we'll relate to him, this dynamic is a beautiful thing. Why? Because when we completely surrender ourselves to our heavenly Father, we sign up for maximum impact in life.

In his wonderfully proactive way, God says to us, "My job is to lead, and your job is to follow. I've already mapped out the steps you should take." And marvelously, those steps lead us to ultimate fulfillment, to his purposes for us . . . to his peace. I often tell newcomers to faith that God chooses for us what we would choose for ourselves, if only we knew what to choose! The psalmist David seemed to understand this: "He leads me beside still waters," he said of God. "He restores my soul. He leads me in paths of righteousness for his name's sake" (Psalm 23:2–3).

God loves his people with an "everlasting love," the prophet tells us in Jeremiah 31:3. His guidance in our lives makes good on that lofty promise. What a good, good Father we serve.

"Thank you for providing for me . . ."

Back to verse 1 of our psalm, David acknowledges that because of God's shepherding over his life, he has no lingering wants or needs. Now, I want us to think about this for a moment. If I were to ask you what you want these days, my guess is that in response you could talk uninterrupted for ten minutes straight before it occurred to you to breathe. There's. Just. So. Much. We. Want.

Beyond our *external* needs for food and shelter and water, we want the stuff that "everyone" seems to have. We want the latest-version iPhone. We want the upgraded kitchen countertops. We want the faster Wi-Fi connection. We want our favorite team to win.

We want things that address our *internal* needs as well: We want purpose in life, and respect from our family members and friends, and happiness, and the delight of getting lost in a good book. We want the feeling of satisfaction that comes from completing a meaningful project. We want intimacy with our spouse. We want joy in our homes. We want to binge-watch the show that people can't quit talking about. We want stimulation and success and support and rest.

And what about our *eternal* needs? God has set eternity in our hearts, according to Ecclesiastes 3:11, which means that you and I arrive on this planet fitted for forgiveness and salvation and a little thing called communion with God.

Considered together, it's a lot to long for. Indeed, we want all these things, and always we want more. For this reason, it can be quite perplexing to come to a verse such as Romans 8:32, which says, "He who did not spare his own Son but gave him up for us all, how will he not also with him graciously give us all things?"

Or John 15:7, which says, "If you abide in me, and my words abide in you, ask whatever you wish, and it will be done for you."

Or Mark 11:24, which says, "Therefore I tell you, whatever you ask in prayer, believe that you have received it, and it will be yours."

Or Psalm 37:4, which says, "Delight yourself in the LORD, and he will give you the desires of your heart."

Or Psalm 84:11, which says, "The LORD God is a sun and a shield; the LORD gives grace and glory; no good thing does He withhold from those who walk uprightly" (NASB).

Or Matthew 7:7, which says, "Ask, and it will be given to you; seek, and you will find; knock, and it will be opened to you."

Are we really supposed to believe that by bringing our list of wants to Jesus, it will actually get checked off somehow?

It's perhaps the greatest *aha* of the Christ-following life, this realization that when we find our satisfaction in Jesus, all worldly wishes fade to gray. The truth of the matter is that behind every other desire is the desire for Jesus. And once we have him, we have everything we could possibly need. In The Living Bible, Psalm 23:1 reads this way: "Because the Lord is my Shepherd, I have everything I need!" (TLB).

"Thank you for protecting me . . ."

A final catalyst for David's gratitude is the Lord's protection in his life. He need not want for community because God is near. He need not want for intimacy because God is personal. He need not want for guidance because God is proactive. He need not want for fulfillment because God is provisional. And he need not want for deliverance because God *protects* him day by day.

"Even though I walk through the valley of the shadow of death," verse 4 reads, "I will fear no evil, for you are with me." You and I understand dark valleys to be times in life when the path is tough to find and the future is uncertain at best, but for David, the Valley of the Shadow was a literal place.

The Wadi Qelt, as it's known, is a tight, twelve-foot-wide canyon beginning in Bethlehem and stretching northward in the West Bank through the Judean desert to Jerusalem. What begins at altitude as a small stream builds strength and velocity as it tumbles downward, eventually dumping into the Dead Sea, the lowest place on earth. This "dumping out into death" is the valley David referred to, a truly treacherous spot for shepherds and their sheep. Not only would wild animals slip into these dimly lit shadowlands, but thieves found the dark and craggy caves to be suitable hiding spots as well.

So yes, while the psalmist's language connotes apt figurative equivalents in our modern minds, this was no hypothetical exercise for David. This valley was *real* for him, just as our valleys are real to us. If you've ever faced a crisis of some sort, be it financial, relational, medical, or otherwise, then you know exactly how David felt. When all around things feel shadowy and uncertain, we desperately need to know that God is near.

These valleys are something we walk *through*. David doesn't speak of camping out in the valley of the shadow of death, despite how the valley of death always feels. No, he says that these places are simply stopovers in life . . . we always make our way through.

A veteran believer was asked about his favorite Scripture passage, to which he responded without hesitation, "The four words, 'It came to pass.'"

Most people I've asked to answer that question pick something a little more familiar. They love John 3:16. Or they love Romans 8:28. Or they love Philippians 4:13. But something as obscure as "It came to pass"? Never had I heard that response. I wondered what it could mean.

"I've seen it time and again in my life," the man continued, "that what comes to pass thankfully never stays. The toughest stuff is blissfully ephemeral: It's here, and then it's gone."

This is a key point for us, my friend. Our problems are real, but they are temporal. *God's blessings* are what stay forever.

The Gifts of Gratitude

In Psalm 23, David demonstrates the second of the three exchanges we can make if our aim is to reignite our spiritual lives. We can exchange doubt for faith, as we saw in chapter 5, and also we can exchange discontentment for gratitude. It is said that gratitude is the expression of appreciation for what one already has, which stands in stark contrast to that pressing urge we talked about previously to crave and acquire and crave and acquire and crave and acquire again. If I were to lay out the justification for living grateful lives, I'd divide my answer in two: First, we practice gratitude because God instructs us to do so; and second, we practice gratitude because grateful people live healthier lives. Let's touch on each reason in turn.

God Instructs Us to Be Grateful

In Romans 1, the apostle Paul cautions believers in Rome of the coming wrath against sinful humanity as an urgent plea to follow Christ. "The wrath of God is being revealed from heaven against all the godlessness and wickedness of people, who suppress the truth by their wickedness," he begins, "since what may be known about God has made it plain to them, because God has made it plain to them. For since the creation of the world God's invisible qualities—his eternal power and divine nature—have been clearly seen, being understood from what has been made, so that people are without excuse" (vv. 18–20 NIV). But despite the images of deviance and defiance that may spring to our minds in accordance with such godlessness and wickedness, Paul pins the problem on a far plainer bent: "For although they knew God," he says, "they neither glorified him as God nor gave thanks to him, but their thinking became futile and their foolish hearts were darkened" (v. 21 NIV).

The mark of the unbeliever, according to this champion of our faith? Lack of gratitude—as simple as that.

"Give thanks to the LORD, for he is good," Psalm 107:1–2 tells us to do, "for his steadfast love endures forever! Let the redeemed of the Lord say so, whom he has redeemed from trouble." Later, in verses 8 and 9, the psalmist continues this theme: "Let them thank the LORD for his steadfast love," he writes, "for his wondrous works to the children of man! For he satisfies the longing soul, and the hungry soul he fills with good things."

First Thessalonians 5:18 says we are to "give thanks in all circumstances; for this is the will of God in Christ Jesus for you."

Hebrews 13:15 instructs us to bring "a sacrifice of praise" before the Lord.

Psalm 63:3–4 tells us to praise the Lord because his "steadfast love is better than life."

Psalm 107:22 confirms that believers "sacrifice thank offerings and tell of his [God's] works with songs of joy" (NIV).

Psalm 100:4 reminds us to "enter his gates with thanksgiving, and his courts with praise!"

Time and again, we are commanded to use our words and our bodies and our hearts and our souls and our mouths and our hands to say thank you to holy God. And while such expressions of gratitude surely warm the heart of our heavenly Father, they serve another purpose in that they hearten his followers too.

Grateful People Live Healthier Lives

I believe it was pioneering twentieth-century Hungarian-Canadian endocrinologist and father of modern stress theory Hans Selye who wrote that "Gratitude produces more positive emotional energy than any other attitude in your life," and since his research days, the body of work has multiplied claiming that gratitude is good for you and me. Years ago, a writer for *Forbes* culled several scientific studies for the seven key benefits of thankfulness, which included both a qualitative and quantitative uptick in one's circle of friends, improved physical health, better emotional stability, an increased sense of empathy, better self-esteem, and ampler mental strength.[2]

But who needs science to understand what we observe empirically in our lives? When we express gratitude, we feel better. Life gets better every time we say thanks. Gratitude "dissolves doubt, reinforces faith, and restores joy," said Ruth Graham, wife of the late evangelist Billy Graham.[3] Indeed, to neglect gratitude is to neglect God's blessing in and over our lives. It's to quite literally fence in our lives. But when we take our eyes off the things going wrong and choose to be grateful for all that is right, we set ourselves up for strength and stability on every conceivable front. We satisfy the commands of our Father, and he makes strong every weakness in our lives.

Making the Trade

In coaching others (not to mention myself) toward this great exchange—laying down discontentment, picking up gratitude instead—I find that vigilance is required. It is said that we humans have a negativity bias, and if you've racked up more than a couple of decades of living on this earth, then you know this to be the case: Despite all the good to be found in the world, sometimes it's just easier to complain. If you'd like to move past this very natural tendency and learn to let thankfulness have its way, then let me give you the same pep talk I often have to give to myself, which centers on three don'ts and a couple of dos.

Don't Be Careless

The first don't is *Don't be careless*. On a clear night, when the stars seem brighter than usual and the moon is a floodlight that feels close at hand, I try to stop whatever I'm doing and thank God for his creative expertise. I do this because on far too many occasions, I glance up at nature's grandeur and carelessly walk on by. Think of it: If we were able to see the stars in the night sky only once or twice a year, we'd structure entire events around those evenings. They'd be special; they'd *matter* to us. The reason we don't hold such gatherings, despite frequently stunning skies, is that we've somehow grown accustomed to our surroundings. To put it bluntly, *we just don't care*.

When God's nation of Israel was stranded in the desert for forty years, God provided nourishment for them in the form of manna. These bread-like flakes would literally fall from heaven in the morning so that the Hebrew people would be able to eat, but after some time, this provision was rejected. "We're sick of this!" his people cried.

Getting the equivalent of divine room service each morning was hardly something to whine about, and yet carelessness caused God's chosen people to lose their powers of observation for this supernatural blessing in their lives.

You and I can be careless too, you know. As I say: To embrace a life of gratitude, vigilance is required.

Don't Be Critical

The second don't is *Don't let a critical spirit seep in*. A critical spirit says, "I will never be satisfied." This isn't a statement of fact, you understand, but rather a statement of will. When you opt for criticism, you *will* yourself to be discontent, deciding to lose the roses and hold fast to the thorns. "In our daily life we long for the way things used to be or the way we want things to be," writes Meredith McDaniel, "and in the middle of it all we miss out on what is right in front of us. We are blinded to the goodness of the moment because we are too busy looking ahead at what could be or grappling with what we do not yet have."[4]

"In everything by prayer and supplication with thanksgiving," Paul writes in Philippians 4:6–7, "let your requests be made known to God. And the peace of God, which surpasses all understanding, will guard your hearts and your minds in Christ Jesus." We mustn't miss that little phrase "with thanksgiving."

With thanksgiving holds the key.

Don't Be Conceited

The third don't is *Don't become conceited*. Not only does pride come before the fall, as Proverbs 16:18 promises, but pride also comes before a great deal of disappointment. The reason for this is that pride is the polar opposite of praise, and as we've established already, ingratitude signals unbelief. When we cease believing God, we cease living in the abundance he created us to enjoy.

146

If your thoughts tend to center on you and yourself alone, look out: Conceit is taking hold. Look out and then quickly look up, for God stands ready to broaden your view. Now, on to the two dos.

Think and Thank

The etymologies of the words *think* (Old Saxon *thenkian*, meaning "to remember or meditate") and *thank* (Old Saxon *thancon*, meaning "to remember or recompense") are so similar as to be nearly indistinguishable from each other, which really aids the follower of Christ. As we *think* about God, we are prompted to *thank* God, to let gratitude flow in our hearts. Similarly, "gratitude" and "grace" derive from the same root.

Contemplate the goodness of God. Remember his faithfulness. Celebrate what Jesus has done for you. An old gospel chorus says, "Thank you, Lord, for saving my soul . . . Thank you, Lord, for giving to me thy great salvation, so rich and free."[5] When we think about the rescue we've been given in Jesus Christ, how can we not feel thankful? Further, how can we not say thanks?

Speak and Sing

If you've familiarized yourself with the Bible at all, then you've probably come across the story in Luke's gospel regarding the ten lepers whom Jesus healed. The story reads as follows:

On the way to Jerusalem he [Jesus] was passing along between Samaria and Galilee. And as he entered a village, he was met by ten lepers, who stood at a distance and lifted up their voices, saying, "Jesus, Master, have mercy on us." When he saw them he said to them, "Go and show yourselves to the priests." And as they went they were cleansed. Then one of them, when he saw that he was healed, turned back, praising God with a loud voice; and he fell on his face at Jesus' feet, giving him thanks. Now he was a Samaritan. Then Jesus answered, "Were not ten cleansed? Where are the nine?

Was no one found to return and give praise to God except this foreigner?" And he said to him, "Rise and go your way; your faith has made you well."

Luke 17:11–19

Those first two questions of Jesus get me every time: "Were not ten cleansed? Where are the nine?"

It's one thing to feel grateful to Jesus—for his protection, for his provision, for his care—but quite another altogether to *speak those words aloud*. People who study quantum physics professionally tell us that you and I are simply bundles of vibrations, reverberating all over the place. It's like we emit radio waves in huge, concentric circles that bounce off everything we come near. It stands to reason, then, that when we allow the thankfulness that we feel to emerge audibly through our lips, we change the order of things for the better by sending positive vibes into our sphere.

If you don't believe me, try it! Stop reading for a few moments and go tell someone how thankful you are for them.

Well, did you do it?

How did you feel as a result?

In the verses we looked at earlier, we saw that the Bible tells us to speak out our praise and also to *sing* to the Lord. Worship always lifts us up. When we lift God up, we are lifted up too!

You'll recall that in the New Testament book of Acts, Luke recounts an episode involving Peter and Silas, disciples of Jesus who were unjustly apprehended and unceremoniously thrown in jail. After the rulers in Philippi had "inflicted many blows upon them," the text says, "they threw them into prison, ordering the jailer to keep them safely" (Acts 16:23).

Later that evening, Paul and Silas were passing the time praying and singing hymns to God. Besides the other prisoners listening to the faithful men sing, the jailer heard them too. And as everyone listened with rapt attention, an earthquake shook the place, releasing the prison doors that held them in. "Sirs, what must I do to be saved?" the jailer asked the men (v. 30), after realizing that their God had sprung them free from that place. The jailer had been on the verge of killing himself, his grief over his negligence so deep. What kind of jailer can't keep his men in jail? But then Paul cried out, "Do not harm yourself, for we are all here" (v. 28).

"Believe in the Lord Jesus," Paul then told him, "and you will be saved, you and your household" (v. 31). He and his loved ones were baptized that very night, the text says, as he entered the family of faith. God inhabits the praises of his people, Psalm 22:3 promises us. As we praise him, his power is made known.

The scene involving the jailer's conversion ought to be instructive for us, not only because we see what's possible when we simply articulate our gratitude to God but also because we are reminded that when we live as thankful people, we always have a testimony to share. Years ago, my friend Brent Trammel was diagnosed with brain cancer, and for more than seventy months he underwent chemo and radiation treatments, just an agonizing course of care. But through it all, I watched this man not merely trust God, but *thank* God sincerely too.

On one occasion, just hours after one of Brent's surgeries, my friend looked at me with a genuine grin and said, "God is so faithful to me. . . ."

He went on to talk in whispered tones, his body worn out from the day, about how thankful he was for God's grace, for salvation, for divine resources when the natural self gives out. I left the hospital that evening thinking, *What a beam of light for the Lord this man is.*

Gratitude has that effect.

The good news I have for you today is that as you begin to trade discontentment for gratitude, you'll enjoy each blessing in your life at least three times. You'll enjoy the blessing of receiving from God and then the blessing of telling him so. As if that weren't delightful enough on its own, you'll then enjoy recounting that blessing for someone else. We can bless others with our gratitude when we remember that all good things come from God.

7

Exchanging Distress for Peace

We must do our business faithfully, without trouble or disquiet; recalling our mind to GOD mildly, and with tranquility, as often as we find it wandering from him.

Brother Lawrence, *The Practice of the Presence of God*

Some wandered in desert wastes, finding no way to a city to dwell in; hungry and thirsty, their soul fainted within them. Then they cried to the LORD in their trouble, and he delivered them from their distress. He led them by a straight way till they reached a city to dwell in. Let them thank the LORD for his steadfast love, for his wondrous works to the children of man! For he satisfies the longing soul, and the hungry soul he fills with good things.

Psalm 107:4–9

On to our third and final exchange. In anticipation of a re-ignited faith, we can trade doubt for faith, which reminds us that God is at hand. We can trade discontentment for gratitude, which reminds us that God is at work. And we can trade distress for peace, which reminds us that despite the mayhem surrounding us, God is *sovereign over all*. When men and women of old "cried to the LORD in their trouble," Psalm 107:6 says, "he delivered them from their distress." The people of God need not suffer in silence; as Scripture upon Scripture testifies, tranquility awaits us all.

The gospel of Mark, chapter 4. As evening fell, Jesus and his disciples decided to cross to the other side of the Sea of Galilee. The sea is situated in a valley in northern Israel, which means the rather tranquil waters can become a tempest in a teapot and fast. As the boat made its way across the expanse, a violent windstorm arose, causing the waves to overtake the craft that was now being submerged.

"Teacher!" the disciples cried out to Jesus, who happened to be snoozing in the stern. "Do you not care that we are perishing?" *Don't you care about us at all?*

"And he awoke and rebuked the wind and said to the sea, 'Peace! Be still!'" (see vv. 35–39).

The wind ceased.

The sea calmed.

Deliverance followed distress.

The gospel of Luke, chapter 8. Jesus and his closest friends were in the country of the Gerasenes when approached by a man who "had demons," as the text says (v. 27). This man was clearly troubled—wearing no clothing, bound by chains, living among tombs. But when he saw Jesus, he fell to his knees and cried out to the Messiah, "Please! Do not torment me!"

Jesus asked the man for his name, to which the demons inside him replied. "Legion," they told Jesus, meaning *many*. "Please don't consign us to the abyss."

Their preferred destination instead, you ask? A filthy herd of pigs. Those pigs, once possessed, rushed over a cliff right into a lake, and the troubled man was made whole. He "went away, proclaiming throughout the whole city how much Jesus had done for him" (v. 39).

Satan's work was contained.

A man's torment was relieved.

Deliverance in response to distress.

The gospel of Mark, chapter 5. Jesus was on his way to heal a man's daughter, and he had garnered quite a crowd. A woman who had been suffering in menstrual pain for twelve years—for whom no doctor could provide a diagnosis and whose issue no amount of money could resolve—approached Jesus and grazed the edge of his garment with her believing, faith-filled hand. "If I touch even his garments, I will be made well," she said, and to no one's surprise she was right.

"Who touched my garments?" Jesus asked, to which the woman came forward, trembling with fear, and admitted what she had done.

"As soon as I touched your clothing," she said, "my flow of blood dried up."

It was her faith that had made her well, and Jesus said to the woman, "Go in peace. Go, and be healed."

Divine power flowed.

A gut-wrenched woman was healed.

Deliverance, just after distress.

The gospel of John, chapter 18. Jesus and his disciples had come to the garden of Gethsemane, where he would pray to the Father just before his arrest and crucifixion . . . just before the most devastating of days. Judas, one of his beloved followers, had just betrayed him, and here came the chief priests and officials, weapons and torches in hand.

After asking for whom the men have come, Jesus stepped forward: "I am he." But Simon Peter wasn't so eager for this plan to unfold. In one swift move, he drew his sword from its sheath and struck the high priest's servant Malchus, severing his ear clean from the side of his head.

Despite the imminent tragedy facing him, Jesus healed Malchus's ear with compassion to spare. "Shall I not drink the cup that the Father has given me?" he says (v. 11). *Shall I not face this thing I must face?*

A wrong was made right.

A pattern was confirmed.

Deliverance, on the heels of distress.

"The effect of righteousness will be peace," said the prophet Isaiah, "and the result of righteousness, quietness and trust forever" (Isaiah 32:17). This effect, this result, is one we desperately need. Our distress is in search of this peace.

In 1914, after the outbreak of World War I, social commentator H. G. Wells wrote a series of articles for various London newspapers that eventually became the backbone of a book titled *The War That Will End War*. In the United States, a variation on that title was later used by President Woodrow Wilson when he addressed the American people in 1917 regarding his decision to enter the war. This would be "the war to end all wars," he said, hoping to assure the public that our country's participation on behalf of world freedom now would mean such participation would never be needed again. Twenty-two years later, the Second World War had begun. And from 1945, when the Second World War ended, until today, to scroll through the list of armed conflicts, rebellions, and outright wars is to come away bleary-eyed and deeply dismayed: leader after enraged leader, skirmish after unresolved skirmish, resolution after rejected resolution, undeniable dearth of peace. Today, in a time of relative peace, still we recognize "10 official wars and 8 active military conflicts,"[1] which supports the understandable suspicion that *no* war will end all wars.

Broadening our definition of war to the metaphoric, we see the same natural disasters, demonic forces, medical quandaries, and emotional outbursts today that were present in Jesus' day, and based on Jesus' counsel to his disciples in the first century—and by extension to us here and now—it's a safe bet that the perils we've known thus far will be with us right to the end. From Matthew 24:3–14:

> As he sat on the Mount of Olives, the disciples came to him privately, saying, "Tell us, when will these things be, and what will be the sign of your coming and of the end of the age?" And Jesus answered them, "See that no one leads you astray. For many will come in my name, saying, 'I am the Christ,' and they will lead many astray. And you will hear of wars and rumors of wars. See that you are not alarmed, for this must take place, but the end is not yet. For nation will rise against nation, and kingdom against kingdom, and there will be famines and earthquakes in various places. All these are but the beginning of the birth pains.
>
> "Then they will deliver you up to tribulation and put you to death, and you will be hated by all nations for my name's sake. And then many will fall away and betray one another and hate one another. And many false prophets will arise and lead many astray. And because lawlessness will be increased, the love of many will grow cold. But the one who endures to the end will be saved. And this gospel of the kingdom will be proclaimed throughout the whole world as a testimony to all nations, and then the end will come."

This idea of lawlessness increasing as "the end" nears is becoming easier and easier to imagine—at least from where I sit today. In most major cities in our country, protesters are working to defund our police departments, believing that lawlessness is a better option for society than the form of law and order practiced today. Time will tell what becomes of the dispute, but for most people my age, the mere notion would have been unthinkable even a year ago. Despite undeniable progress being made generation after generation with respect to eradicating slavery, slashing global poverty, and seeing countless millions come to Christ, so many trends we're seeing still today leave us shaking our heads in despair: school shootings; church shootings; the attacks on traditional marriage; the rise of terrorist activity both in the United States and abroad;

the practice of abortion; persistent sins of racism in our melting pot of a nation, leading to our cities being set ablaze. "Can things get any worse?" those who are paying attention keep asking me, which is an understandable question to pose. Doesn't God see us here in our suffering? Doesn't he long to come to our aid?

Just after Jesus' triumphal entry into Jerusalem, where he would face crucifixion for the sins of humankind, he gathered his closest followers together and told them of events that were to come. In the gospel of John, chapters 13 through 17, we read what is considered the last will and testament of our Lord, those things that as believers we've been bequeathed. What would Jesus choose to focus on? What would be deemed most important for him to convey? Knowing the suffering that awaited him, what would he choose to say?

There in the upper room, Jesus washed his disciples' feet. He shared a Communion meal with them. He gave them a new commandment to love one another. He promised a Helper would come. And then he told them he had a gift for them that would help them to live stable and satisfied lives. What was this gift? Was it financial security or perpetual good health? What about conflict-free relationships? Vocational achievement? Intelligence? Charm?

The gift, it turns out, was *peace*. "Peace I leave with you; my peace I give to you," he said to them in John 14:27. "Not as the world gives do I give to you. Let not your hearts be troubled, neither let them be afraid."

If you've ever visited the magnificent land of Israel, then you've heard the greeting "Shalom," which means *peace to you* or *serenity to you*. The word is an offering of well-being from one person to another, of stability, of security, of the sense that all is right. The gift that Jesus gave to his disciples—and to us—was not the absence of conflict, but rather the constant presence of Christ. It was the inner reality that all was well despite outward unwellness on the move. "When peace like a river attendeth my way," wrote hymn writer Horatio Spafford after losing his daughters to a horrific trans-Atlantic accident at sea, "when sorrows like sea billows roll; whatever my lot, Thou hast taught me to know it is well, it is well, with my soul."[2]

What Spafford's words remind us is that, in Jesus, the deliverance we long for we already hold in our hands.

"My peace . . ."

To grasp the magnitude of the gift Jesus handed to his disciples prior to facing the cross, we would do well to slow down and scrutinize each of the phrases he spoke. "My peace I give to you," he said. Let's start with whose peace it was.

Throughout Scripture, we find prolific proof that Jesus is not only the Son of God but also, as the second person of the Trinity, is *himself* God. In John 10:30, Jesus says, "The Father and I are one" (NLT). The apostle Paul, writing in Philippians 2:6, exhorts the believers at Philippi to have the same attitude as Christ Jesus, "who, though he was in the form of God, did not count equality with God a thing to be grasped." Writing in Colossians 2:9–10, he reminds believers that "in him [Jesus] the whole fullness of deity dwells bodily, and you have been filled in him, who is the head of all rule and authority."

In John 17:21, we read a portion of Jesus' prayer to the Father in which he asks "that they [believers] may all be one, just as you, Father, are in me, and I in you, that they also may be in us, so that the world may believe that you have sent me."

Earlier in the gospel of John, John says that "in the beginning was the Word [Jesus], and the Word was with God, and the Word was God" (John 1:1); that "the Word became flesh and dwelt among us, and we have seen his glory, glory as of the only Son from the Father, full of grace and truth" (John 1:14); and that "no one has ever seen God; the only God, who is at the Father's side, he has made him known" (John 1:18).

Finally, leaving no room for ambiguity, in John 5:19, Jesus tells his followers, "Truly, truly, I say to you, the Son can do nothing of his own accord, but only what he sees the Father doing. For whatever the Father does, that the Son does likewise."

The point of this quick review? It's that only Jesus can broker the peace of God for us, because without Jesus, we remain separated from God. The secret to Jesus' peace was his eternal fellowship with the Father. When we welcome Jesus, we welcome his peace, and his peace is the peace of God. I am staking my life and eternity on Jesus being God, and on his peace bringing me peace with God, both now and forever.

"I give . . ."

Next, we acknowledge that the peace we desire is the peace that Christ gives, not the peace we find in the world. The peace we find in Jesus is the only perfect peace.

My friend Dan Southern, past president of the American Tract Society, located in Dallas, relayed a story to me of a man he worked with who had visited the famed Peace Palace in The Hague, the Netherlands. This massive building, funded by the [Andrew] Carnegie Foundation and completed just before the outbreak of World War I, houses not only the International Court of Justice and the Permanent Court of Arbitration but also what's known as the Peace Palace Library, which houses more than one million titles, all of which relate to the topic of peace.

Dan said to me, "So, my colleague was talking to a woman who worked at the Peace Palace, and she said proudly, 'We have every book published on the subject of peace in our collection.' He said, 'Oh! Do you have Billy Graham's book *Peace with God*?' to which she replied, 'Well, no, we don't have that one.' He said,

'Do you have the one from Charles Stanley, *Finding Peace*, or Ken Sande's bestseller, *The Peacemaker*?'"

The woman sheepishly shook her head. Feeling a little bad for grilling her, Dan's colleague decided to throw her a nice easy pitch, straight down the middle. "Surely you at least have a Bible here, don't you?"

To the woman's credit, she eventually did produce a Bible, but only after excusing herself, heading to a back room, fumbling through a tall stack of shelves, and locating a Middle Ages relic being kept in storage.

A *million* titles in the Peace Palace Library, and all but one of them mere facsimiles of true peace. Listen, if we could have achieved true peace through military prowess, don't you think we'd have world peace by now? If true peace could be achieved through financial success, wouldn't we have world peace by now? If we could get to a place of peace via political scheming, wouldn't we have *plenty* of peace by now?

I was a child of the 1960s, and if ever there were a generation committed to the prospect of peace, it was mine. A young generation sang about peace, shouted for peace, and protested in favor of peace. "Give peace a chance!" was the cry, desperate to address the rampant chaos in the world. But only those of us who found our way to Jesus would have that deep need met. Why? Because only Jesus can give us true peace.

"to you."

"My peace," Jesus says, "I give *to you*." Which means that for those of us who are "in Christ," we are possessors of this peace. We may choose peace whenever we're distressed—today, here and now, always. The prophet Isaiah reminds us that God will "keep him in perfect peace whose mind is stayed on you, because he trusts in you" (Isaiah 26:3). When we stay focused on God, trusting fully in God, we access the peace that in Christ is ours.

Accepting Christ's Offer of Peace

We need peace. We *want* peace. We have access to peace through Christ. But how do we apprehend this peace we desire? How do we become *people of peace*?

Seek Peace

In the third chapter of the Old Testament book of Daniel, we encounter three young Hebrew men who refused to bow down to the king of Babylon's image and thus defy their allegiance to Jehovah God and as punishment were thrown into a fiery furnace. The king's servants heated the furnace to seven times its normal temperature, and yet when they observed Shadrach, Meshach, and Abednego, who were bound by ropes to the walls of the cavernous pit, they noticed that while their cords of restraint were being incinerated, the men were not being burned. Alarmed by this foiling of his evil plot, the king himself, King Nebuchadnezzar, decided to have a look, which is when he saw not three bodies, but four, in his furnace. *Four?* he wondered. *Why were there four?*

"Who is the god who will deliver you out of my hands?" the king had asked the three, just before having them tossed into the pit, to which they'd replied, "O Nebuchadnezzar, we have no need to answer you in this matter. If this be so, our God whom we serve is able to deliver us from the burning fiery furnace, and he will deliver us out of your hand, O king. But if not, be it known to you, O king, that we will not serve your gods or worship the golden image that you have set up" (Daniel 3:15, 16–18).

I don't know about you, but had I been in the fire that day, I think I would have focused on a few other things—flames and heat certainly come to mind. What Shadrach, Meshach, and Abednego seemed to apprehend that I might have been slower to seize was that fixating on the fire would have done nothing but choke out hope. In terms of its old Anglo-Saxon derivation, the word for *worry* means "to choke." The word is *wurgen*, and the image it would have connoted to the ancient mind was that of a wolf at the throat of its prey. Still today, whenever we choose to worry, we're allowing our emotions to strangle us cold.

It has been said that people living in the United States are among the most fretful people on earth, and based on my empirical observations during my travels around the globe, I would tend to agree with that assessment. We are a nation that prizes speed and output, and we never know when to stop. We're burdened, we're broken, we're overwhelmed, and we're tired. And yet we keep running, and pushing, and fighting, and hoping that we'll someday reach the finish line. The only problem I see is that we keep moving that line! Enough is just never enough.

So when most Americans I know—myself included—read a story like the one about Shadrach, Meshach, and Abednego and learn that those men didn't fixate on the fire, our minds explode in awe: *Is it even possible to live like that?*

Jesus seemed to think so. He said in Matthew 6:25–32 during his famed Sermon on the Mount,

"Therefore I tell you, do not be anxious about your life, what you will eat or what you will drink, nor about your body, what you will put on. Is not life more than food, and the body more than clothing? Look at the birds of the air: they neither sow nor reap nor gather into barns, and yet your heavenly Father feeds them. Are you not of more value than they? And which of you by being anxious can add a single hour to his span of life? And why are you anxious about clothing? Consider the lilies of the field, how they grow: they neither toil nor spin, yet I tell you, even Solomon in all his glory was not arrayed like one of these. But if God so clothes the grass of the field, which today is alive and tomorrow is thrown into the oven, will he not much more clothe you, O you of little faith? Therefore do not be anxious, saying, 'What shall we eat?' or 'What shall we drink?' or 'What shall we wear?' For the Gentiles seek after all these things, and your heavenly Father knows that you need them all."

161

So if we are not to be anxious, then what *are* we to do? Verse 33: "But seek first the kingdom of God and his righteousness, and all these things will be added to you."

I think back to that passage that was pinned to the bulletin board in my childhood bedroom, which began, "Trust in the LORD with all your heart, and do not lean on your own understanding" (Proverbs 3:5), and see that the phrasing of that command implies that *another understanding exists*. God longs for us to pursue *his* understanding of a given matter, not our own. Pastor Chuck Swindoll, in his commentary on Proverbs, writes of chapter 3, verses 5 and 6, "Throw yourself completely upon the Lord. Cast all your present and future needs on Him who is your intimate Savior-God . . . and find in him your security and safety. Do this with all your mind and feeling and will. In order to make this possible, you must refuse to support yourself upon the crutch of human ingenuity. Instead, study the Lord. Learn about His character, discover His plans for you and the world, be amazed by His love and concern for you in each one of your circumstances. Then He—having been granted full control of your life—will smooth out and make straight your paths, removing obstacles along the way."[3]

A smoothed-out, straightened path . . . I defy you to choke on that.

Seek the Lord. Seek his righteousness. Seek the unity found only in him. Quit fixating on all that could go wrong or is in this very moment going wrong. Fixate on peace instead. Consider your heavenly Father who cares both for the flowers of the field and for the birds of the air. Let go of your identity as a worrier and become a worshiper instead. "Perfect love casts out fear," 1 John 4:18 says, which means that when you and I align ourselves with the One who can indeed love perfectly, our heavenly Father, we will in that moment know no fear. We will know no chaos. We will know no disorder. We will know no strife.

We find what it is we're looking for. To our subject at hand, look for peace.

Make Peace

It probably won't surprise you to learn that a passage on overcoming anxiety is among the top ten most commonly searched Bible passages online.[4] In Philippians 4:6–7, which we looked at in an earlier chapter, the apostle Paul exhorts believers to be anxious for nothing, but instead to let our requests be made known to God so that his peace, which passes understanding, will keep charge over our hearts and minds. And if anyone could speak to this idea of living from a place of peace despite chaotic circumstances all around, it certainly was the apostle Paul, who penned those words from a Roman prison cell, serving his sentence for preaching Christ.

There are prison cells of personal suffering and chronic sickness. There are prison cells of moral failure and financial defeat. There are prison cells of relational upheaval and outright depression. There are prison cells of loneliness and fear. But to them all, it's as if Paul were saying, "Whatever prison you find yourself in, *the peace of God can be yours.*" Despite Paul's upsetting present and his uncertain future, he was determined to trust God's plans for him. He was determined to stay steadfast and strong. He was determined to look up instead of looking around. He was determined to practice peace.

It's worth noting that in describing the peace of Jesus, Paul uses the Greek word *eirene*, which means "to come together" or "to reconcile," and each time my studies bring me to that passage in Philippians 4, a memory comes to mind. I was a young pastor, perhaps twenty-eight years of age, and I had been asked to counsel a couple who were having marital disputes. The man and his wife arrived at my office with their blond four-year-old son in tow, and as the couple settled into their seats on the couch that faced me, that little boy wedged himself right between them. I couldn't help but notice that as the husband and wife laid out their struggles, the conversation becoming quite heated at times, the child would quietly and subtly reach for his daddy's right hand and his mommy's left hand and try to get those hands to touch. He'd been caught up in their rumble for far too long, and he was determined to end their fight.

That's the picture that comes to mind when I think of the peace of God: It's togetherness, unity, the visceral experience that *all is well in our world*. It's not merely seeking out order and oneness and calm, but acting on those things we've found. Think of it: If you gave me an expensive gift, and I proceeded never to use it even once, would you believe that I valued that gift? Would you think I had any use for that gift at all?

Jesus paid the ultimate price to secure peace for you and me and asks only that we pick it up and *use* it as we make our way through this life. This is what it is to "make peace"—simply acting on what we know to be true for those who are in Jesus Christ.

When we're at odds with our spouse, we choose to exhale, to let down our defenses, to say, "I want to understand your perspective . . . can you please help me to understand?" We lay down disorder and pick up peace instead, thereby treasuring Jesus' marvelous gift.

When we're tempted to fret over finances, we choose to take our anxious thoughts captive, we rest in God's provision, we stop obsessing about dollars and cents, and we believe that all will be well. We lay down disorder and pick up peace instead, thereby treasuring Jesus' marvelous gift.

When we're despairing over a lost opportunity—in business, in lifestyle, in love—we step back from the edge of the precipice, we remember God's great faithfulness, we set our minds on his goodness, and we agree that better days lie ahead. We lay down disorder and pick up peace instead, thereby treasuring Jesus' marvelous gift.

When we're frustrated over the latest drama regarding our teenager's rebellion, we gather our wits, we manifest not foolishness but wisdom, and we move toward the kid instead of away. We lay down disorder and pick up peace instead, thereby treasuring Jesus' marvelous gift.

Give Peace Away

To fully accept Christ's offer of peace, we *seek* peace. We *make* peace. And finally, we *give peace away*.

Debbie Cowart is a friend from our church who lost her devoted husband, Bret, years ago. Bret was the picture of health: a vibrant man in his thirties, former college baseball player, and fun-loving father to three adventuresome boys. But while the Cowarts were deeply connected to Prestonwood at the time of Bret's death, things weren't always that way.

A member of Prestonwood's men's softball league who was an acquaintance of Bret's and knew of his background playing ball invited Bret to join the league. Bret's high energy, his naturally competitive spirit, and his gregarious personality were a winning combination, and soon enough the other guys took him in like a beloved brother. He thought it was a little odd that following each game, they all huddled together and offered a prayer of thanksgiving for a great evening, but if that's what it took to be part of the league, then so be it. Bret was unfazed. God, however, was at work.

Several weeks into the softball season, one of the other players invited Bret to join him at his men's Bible study one weekday morning, and without really knowing why he said yes, Bret agreed to come. There, after hearing a clear presentation of the gospel, he surrendered his life to Jesus, he began studying Scripture and growing in his faith, and he found himself dreaming of starting a sports ministry for boys who didn't have a dad at home. But then came the cancer diagnosis, and the treatments, and a smidge of progress, only to be followed by terrible regression. Eventually, God called Bret Cowart home.

Following Bret's memorial service, Debbie wrote me a letter, detailing what the entire experience had been like. I have her permission to share this excerpt with you here: "God has given me joy through all of this. I know people don't understand how you can have joy when you've weathered such a loss. They certainly don't understand how you can have peace in the midst of peril. But I'm here to tell you that you can.

"Our families were so concerned about leaving the boys and me down here in Texas by ourselves, but after they saw the love that was shown to us by our church family, they realized we were in good hands. We could not have gotten through all of this if it weren't for the body of Christ, the church. God has been so good to us."

When we seek peace and make peace, we then have peace to offer the world. We become peacemakers—people who bring peace with them wherever they go, people who help others to look beyond their harrowing circumstances to see the hallowed ground on which they stand. Trials and tribulations are opportunities to come nearer to the One—the *only* One—who can truly help us overcome them. When you are a person of peace, boundless opportunities exist all around you for helping others also to live at ease.

A Life Lived at Ease

I want to leave you with a picture from the well-known Old Testament chapter of Psalm 46. There, the psalmist—one of the "three sons of Korah," perhaps King Hezekiah, perhaps the prophet Isaiah—wrote, "God is our refuge and strength, a very present help in trouble. Therefore we will not fear though the earth gives way, though the mountains be moved into the heart of the sea, though its waters roar and foam, though the mountains tremble at its swelling" (vv. 1–3).

In verses 10 and 11, he continues, speaking on behalf of God, "'Be still, and know that I am God. I will be exalted among the nations, I will be exalted in the earth!' The LORD of hosts is with us; the God of Jacob is our fortress."

Now, most likely, if you've been walking with Jesus for any significant length of time, then you've read the words of that psalm many times before. What may be new to you is the context within which they were written. For a Middle Easterner, these would have been distressing times as the Assyrian army marched its way across the land, decimating everything in its path. The next target on their hit list was the city of Jerusalem, and King Hezekiah, a good and godly king ruling over *all* of Judea, was none too pleased. But what was he to do? His task was equivalent to you or me stopping the malicious activities of modern-day ISIS. In the king's view, there was no hope.

To further stoke Hezekiah's fear, the Assyrian King Sennacherib sent him a letter, telling him to surrender at once or else die. Despite the temptation to cave under pressure, Hezekiah took the letter into the temple, the place of worship, and laid it out before the Lord. "O LORD of hosts," he prayed, "God of Israel, enthroned above the cherubim, you are the God, you alone, of all the kingdoms of the earth; you have made heaven and earth. Incline your ear, O LORD, and hear; open your eyes, O LORD, and see; and hear all the words of Sennacherib, which he has sent to mock the living God. Truly, O LORD, the kings of Assyria have laid waste all the nations and their lands, and have cast their gods into the fire. For they were no gods, but the work of men's hands, wood and stone. Therefore they were destroyed. So now, O LORD our God, save us from his hand, that all the kingdoms of the earth may know that you alone are the LORD" (Isaiah 37:16–20).

That night, despite his heartfelt prayer to God, Hezekiah probably went to bed believing in his heart of hearts that the end was near for his land. Have you ever felt that way? You so badly want to believe that God will show up for you, even as you harbor some *serious* doubts.

As it turned out, those doubts proved baseless. Did the Lord *ever* show up that night.

Isaiah chapter 37, verse 36 says, "And the angel of the LORD went out and struck down 185,000 in the camp of the Assyrians. And when people arose early in the morning, behold, these were all dead bodies." The text goes on to report that the king of Assyria, who survived the attack, went home to Nineveh and was worshiping his god Nisroch when his two sons struck him down with a sword so that they could assume his throne.

This is what we call a bad day for Assyria, right? But it made for a very good day for our king.

That imagery of God being a *fortress* is key for you and me, because there is plenty about life in this world today that will make us feel unsafe. Each decade that passes confirms what Jesus promised us would be true, which is that in this world, we will have trouble. I see plenty of trouble; don't you? And yet here is what he wanted us to know: *He has overcome this world*.

We ought to tattoo that picture of the mighty Assyrian army being leveled by the angel of the Lord onto our minds and hearts so that we never live a single day apart from the reminder that it brings. God really is greater than he that is in the world. He really is greater than any amount of human force this world cares to throw our way.

God is our help in times of trouble.

God is our refuge from every storm.

God is our citadel, our castle.

God is our surefire place to run to.

He is our fortress.

He is our protection.

He is our cover.

He is our wing.

He is our peace amid life's frenzied tumult.

He is *all-rightness* on all days in all ways.

PART THREE

Results of Going with God

8

Wanting What God Wants

The whole duty of man is summed up in obedience to God's will.

Attributed to George Washington

Now may the God of peace who brought again from the dead our Lord Jesus, the great shepherd of the sheep, by the blood of the eternal covenant, equip you with everything good that you may do his will, working in us that which is pleasing in his sight, through Jesus Christ, to whom be glory forever and ever. Amen.

Hebrews 13:20–21

Here we begin a discussion on the four magnificent benefits of having a reignited faith. Around Prestonwood, I often remind fellow worshipers that while God exists outside of any formula we might care to force him into, there is an equation I've seen play out time and again in my life and in the lives of those I pastor. In fact, I've never *not* seen it to be true. The formula is this:

Dedication + Transformation = Reignition

171

In Parts 1 and 2 of this book, we looked at both the *traditions*—reading and living according to God's Word, engaging with God in prayer, connecting with the broader body of believers, and operating from the place of victory that is ours in Jesus Christ—and the *trades*—exchanging doubt for faith, discontentment for gratitude, and distress for peace—that mark the Christ-following life. Now, in these chapters comprising Part 3, we will explore what we could rightly call the *trends of transformation* that unfold in our lives as we dedicate ourselves to those things. Those trends include the treasuring of God's will instead of our own; the irrepressible tendency to share the good news of the gospel with those who have not yet accepted the gift of grace; persistence in the faith beyond what we think we're capable of; and the eternal enjoyment of God's presence, both as we anticipate the grandeur of heaven and as we usher heavenly realities into our earthly existence, here and now.

The net effect of our dedication to spiritual practices and God's commitment to transform us in these ways? It's the reignited faith we desire.

If there is one subject I have been asked about over the years more than any other, it is the subject of God's will. I once heard it said that life equates to the "C between B and D." Between *birth* and *death* lie *choices*,[1] and depending on the ones we make, we shape a life. So much is riding on our choices that it's no wonder we stress about making the ones that are "right." For the believer, it's effortless to be born (thank you, moms!), and it's elating to be born again (thank you, Jesus!). What seems neither effortless nor elating is the middle; *how do we live rightly in between?*

In this chapter's epigraph from Hebrews 13, we find a benediction of sorts from the writer of Hebrews to Jewish Christians suffering persecution six decades or so after Jesus was crucified and resurrected from the dead. He wanted to remind believers of what was *most important* in staying the course with Christ. Earlier in the chapter, the writer offered a list of wonderful exhortations for how to live uprightly in a world that was spiritually upside down: "Let brotherly love continue," he said. "Do not neglect to show hospitality to strangers, for thereby some have entertained angels unawares. Remember those who are in prison, as though in prison with them, and those who are mistreated, since you also are in the body. Let marriage be held in honor among all, and let the marriage bed be undefiled, for God will judge the sexually immoral and adulterous. Keep your life free from love of money, and be content with what you have, for he has said, 'I will never leave you nor forsake you'" (Hebrews 13:1–5).

"Remember your leaders," he continues, "those who spoke to you the word of God. Consider the outcome of their way of life, and imitate their faith. . . . Do not be led away by diverse and strange teachings, for it is good for the heart to be strengthened by grace, not by foods, which have not benefited those devoted to them. . . . Through him [Jesus] then let us continually offer up a sacrifice of praise to God, that is, the fruit of lips that acknowledge his name. Do not neglect to do good and to share what you have, for such sacrifices are pleasing to God. Obey your leaders and submit to them, for they are keeping watch over your souls, as those who will have to give an account. Let them do this with joy and not with groaning, for that would be of no advantage to you" (vv. 7, 9, 15–17).

It would be easy to point to scriptural passages such as this one whenever I'm asked about "God's will" and say simply, "There. Just go do that." Go love well. Go show hospitality to strangers. Visit those who are in prison. Revere marriage. Don't cheat on your spouse. Don't be greedy, but instead be grateful for the gifts God has given you. Pray for your leaders. Stick to good doctrine. Share what you have. Live well with others, and you'll be good. But while those instructions would indeed align with the teachings of Jesus, they hardly address the nuanced needs people tend to lay at my feet.

Such as, "Is this person the one I should marry?"

"Should I take this job?"

"What do we do about our wayward son?"

"How am I supposed to survive working for my narcissistic boss?"

What these people—and you, perhaps—want to know is how to make the right decisions based on your specific circumstances. What does "God's will" mean, you wonder, as it relates to *your* life, here and now?

In verses 20 and 21 of Hebrews 13, the writer says this: "Now may the God of peace who brought again from the dead our Lord Jesus, the great shepherd of the sheep, by the blood of the eternal covenant, equip you with everything good that you may do his will, working in us that which is pleasing in his sight, through Jesus Christ, to whom be glory forever and ever. Amen."

Here in these words is a powerful truth regarding God's will, which is that rather than it being something you and I have to *seek out*, we need only *surrender* to it. It is God who ushered in peace by raising Jesus from the dead. It is God who equips us with every good thing. It is God—and God alone—who can work in us that which is pleasing in his sight. What is God's will for you and me? It's that we would let him be Lord of our lives.

What God Creates, He Sustains

Historically, there have been two prevailing views on how you and I arrived here on planet Earth. One theory is that we evolved from cosmic goo that spontaneously became ordered, which led to the appearance of sea animals, which became primates, which became us. "Like modern-day apes and monkeys, we evolved from ancient monkeys," writes University of Rhode Island associate professor of anthropology Holly Dunsworth. "And like all vertebrates with four-limbs, known as tetrapods, we evolved from the same ancient fishes."[2] The general thinking here is that nothing times nothing equals everything, math that is impossible to get behind.

But Christians believe something much more reasonable, which is that "in the beginning, God created the heavens and the earth" (Genesis 1:1). The believing Christian knows that God spoke, and the universe was formed, that God was the originator of all we see and experience today, that humankind was *divinely* formed—made in the image of God, no less—and crafted on purpose for an *eternal* purpose.

To follow the pages of Genesis is to see that not long after God created man—and, shortly thereafter, woman—those created beings defied his authority in their lives by eating from the one tree God had forbidden them to eat from, the Tree of the Knowledge of Good and Evil. Upon going their own way instead of God's, they ushered sin into the world. Where there had been no disease, no distortion, no depravity, now those things and more showed up. God's original intent could no longer be fulfilled. Adam and Eve would be expelled from the garden of Eden—from Paradise—never to return again.

And yet even as God removed the crown of his creation from that perfect place, he set in motion his redemptive plan. He would send his Son, Jesus, someday, wrapped in human flesh and anointed to live a sinless life, to enter the earth, to face a brutal death on a cross as payment for humankind's sin, and to rise on the third day as proof that by his great sacrifice all forms of death had been defeated. In that one marvelous event, the separation from God that people had experienced would be bridged. We could commune with God once more.

We take from this story the fact that not only did God *create* us but he *sustained* us by his power and grace. When we say yes to God, we say yes to crossing that Bridge he provided, day after day after day. "Thou hast formed us for Thyself," said Augustine of Hippo, "and our hearts are restless till they find rest in Thee."[3]

Indeed, you and I will never find satisfaction in life until we find ourselves surely surrendered to God.

To revisit that Upper Room Discourse we looked at earlier is to find Jesus boldly declaring this very theme: "Truly, truly, I say to you, whoever believes in me will also do the works that I do; and greater works than these will he do, because I am going to the Father. Whatever you ask in my name, this I will do, that the Father may be glorified in the Son. If you ask me anything in my name, I will do it" (John 14:12–14).

Jesus commits to doing "anything" we ask in his name, a promise that has baffled believers the world over. But if we simply keep reading, we come to understand how he could make such a seemingly wild claim. "If you love me, you will keep my commandments," he said in verse 15. Then, in verse 21, he said, "Whoever has my commandments and keeps them, he it is who loves me. And he who loves me will be loved by my Father, and I will love him and manifest myself to him." Finally, in verses 23 and 24, we read, "If anyone loves me, he will keep my word, and my Father will love him, and we will come to him and make our home with him. Whoever does not love me does not keep my words. And the word that you hear is not mine but the Father's who sent me."

The power point here is this: As we are faithful to love God, to keep the commandments of God, to prioritize the will of God, to faithfully go God's way instead of our own, then whatever we ask in accordance with these things, Jesus will happily do. *Whatever we ask for within the will of God will be done in Jesus' name.*

Which begs the question, of course: What exactly do we mean when we say "the will of God"?

What We Mean When We Say "God's Will"

Since humankind's creation in the garden of Eden, God's intention was to commune with us, to enjoy uninterrupted fellowship with the crown of his creation, his *pièce de résistance*. Once sin entered the world through the disobedience of Adam and Eve, God's mission was broadened to include a plan of redemption to restore what sin had stolen, to reestablish the lines of intimate communication that had been broken by waywardness, willfulness, and greed. At the highest of levels, "God's will" centers on working in and then through the lives of human believers in him to accomplish that redemptive work. We looked previously at the Great Commission, and this is where that commission takes hold: As you and I and millions of others who have surrendered their lives to Jesus go out into our neighborhoods and our communities and our workplaces and our gyms and our local restaurants and shine like stars in the night to the darkened world all around us, preaching the gospel without fear and sharing our testimony without reservation, people are magnetized to this redemptive mission. People surrender their lives to Christ. This overall objective is what we mean when we speak of the "will of God."

Now, if we descend from thirty thousand feet to about fifteen thousand feet, we can start to delineate a couple of different aspects to that overall will. While there are different names for the two parts of God's will that we will address here, it suffices to say that God has a universal or "decretive" will, and God has a moral or "preceptive" will.

God's *decretive will* reflects his unchanging purposes in the universe. He decreed the creation of the earth. He decreed his preeminence and sovereignty over all of life. He decreed the arrival in human flesh of his Son, Jesus. He decreed that all would have the opportunity, through Jesus, to come to God by faith. He has decreed the second coming of Jesus, which has yet to occur. These events cannot be altered, because they have been formally decreed by God.

God also has a moral aspect to his will, which can be called his *preceptive will*. The root there is "precepts," which is another way of referring to principles, edicts, laws, and rules. God's preceptive will reflects the tenets for living he has set forth for humankind.

177

The Ten Commandments are part of God's preceptive will. The "one another" exhortations sprinkled throughout the New Testament are part of God's preceptive will. The injunctions to love and serve God with our heart, soul, mind, and strength are all preceptive in nature.

The reason these distinctions are important to understand is that if you feel stuck and are struggling to understand "God's will for your life," then your starting point is to revisit both God's decretive will and God's preceptive will to see where you may have lost your way. Regarding his decretive will, are you still allowing God to be God in your life? Is Jesus occupying the preeminent position in your life, or have you tried to dethrone him by doing your own thing and going your own way? Are you fully surrendered to know and do his will?

Or what about God's moral will? On so many occasions, people who come to me wanting to know if they should marry a certain person, accept a certain job, move to a certain city, or activate a certain disciplinary plan with their kid have failed to follow the precepts God has set forth in his Word. They aren't reading their Bibles. They aren't prioritizing prayer by staying connected to the Vine, as John 15 says for us to do. They aren't being kind and loving to their neighbors. In many cases, they barely know who their neighbors are!

My point is that God has told us that as we honor his decretive will and surrender to his preceptive will, he will tell us which way to go. He will direct our steps. He will set forth our path. He will lead us onward and upward.

God will not take you and me one step further than the measure of our obedience to him. This means that if we are living in active disobedience to the tenets God *already has set forth*, then why on earth would he give us new, more specific instructions to follow? If your kid, who has never once been on a ski slope, comes to you and says, "I want to be able to do ski jumps like the people I see on TV!" you're probably going to say, "Great! But first, how about a ski lesson? Let's see how you do on the bunny slope."

When we are faithful to do what God already commanded us to do, his direction in our lives will become clearer. "For the LORD God is a sun and shield," Psalm 84:11 says; "the LORD bestows favor and honor. No good thing does he withhold from those who walk uprightly."

Look to Scripture

In terms of how to begin to understand God's will, I already mentioned looking to Scripture. The reason we began our journey together in God's Word is because it is simply impossible to overstate the importance of reading Scripture, meditating on its truths, praying God's Word back to him, and orienting your life around the priorities and principles you find in the pages of the Word of God.

The great twentieth-century American Presbyterian pastor Donald Barnhouse has been quoted as saying that "99 percent of the will of God is above the neck." He meant that as we sanctify our intellect, all of life gets sanctified. When we conform our beliefs to the will of God, our bodies will follow. Such sanctification happens by interacting with the Word of God.

Listen to the Spirit

In addition to reading and living out God's Word, be sure to listen to the Spirit of God. In Romans 8:14, the apostle Paul, writing to believers in Rome, said, "For those who are led by the Spirit of God are the children of God" (NIV).

If you are a believer, then the Holy Spirit of God resides in you and promises to guide you day by day. This is good news! The Holy Spirit will never tell you to do something that God's Word doesn't also lead you to do. Don't expect to break God's commandments and fulfill the will of God. No, the Spirit will *always* agree with God's will.

Long for Serenity

Finally, long for serenity in your life. We spent an entire chapter on exchanging distress for peace, so here I will simply issue the reminder that God's plan for us is peace. When I am walking in God's will, there is stability, not chaos confidence, not doubt; and clarity, not confusion.

Scottish physician and explorer David Livingstone was a great nineteenth-century missionary pioneer whose work culminated in a legacy that was near mythic in status. "In his 30 years of travel and Christian missionary work in southern, central, and eastern Africa—often in places where no European had previously ventured," Britannica cites, "Livingstone may well have influenced Western attitudes toward Africa more than any other individual before him. His discoveries—geographic, technical, medical, and social—provided a complex body of knowledge that is still being explored."[4]

When Livingstone died in 1873, his body was taken back to Europe for burial, but his heart was left in Africa. Isn't that something? African Christians treasured the man's influence so dearly that they insisted on burying his heart in their native soil. As it related to knowing, serving, and defending the Africans he came across, David Livingstone had gone all in.

To properly regard God's will is to similarly go *all in*. It is to say, "God, whatever you're up to in and around me, I am ready. I am here for it. I am in." We are God's "workmanship," Ephesians 2:10 says, the embodied handiwork of the King! As such, our lives only take on significance when we stay safely in the King's hands.

What It's Like Inside God's Will

The peace of God is incomprehensible but unmistakable and undeniable. If you've ever experienced the peace that the apostle Paul describes as "passing understanding" (see Philippians 4:7), then you know that wise people do everything in their power to live in that place of peace. The peace I'm referring to is a key indicator that you are centered in the will of God, that you have forsaken your own whims for "how life should go" and instead are confident in his plans.

During seasons of greatest fruitfulness in my own life—times when I practiced spiritual disciplines with both fervency and frequency, experienced ever-increasing intimacy with Jesus, and saw God use me to effect meaningful change in others' spiritual journeys—this sort of peace was always present, even when circumstances were challenging. Losing my father when I was in my twenties comes to mind, as does having to muddle my way through that year of depression. Staying tethered to God's ways was to eclipse all else with a steadiness that simply couldn't be from me.

In case you're wondering if you are living in God's will here and now, I want to give you three snapshots of the vantage point from there. What's it like inside of God's will? What is true for the follower of Christ?

We Delight in God

When you're squarely in the will of God, you will *delight in God*, which is the first of three snapshots we'll look at.

In the mid-1600s, a group of English and Scottish theologians came together to conform the Church of England to the Church of Scotland. The result of their meeting was the Shorter Westminster Catechism, one of three profound and long-living spiritual documents, the other two being the long form of the catechism and the Westminster Confession.

Despite its name, the Shorter Catechism isn't short at all, but rather comprises a full 107 questions and scripturally based answers about what it means to follow Christ. "What is faith in Jesus Christ?" one of the questions reads. And "What is sanctification?" And "What is forbidden in the tenth commandment?" And "What benefits do believers receive from Christ at the resurrection?" You and I could do far worse than to spend an evening reading the questions and answers as prose; indeed, we would come away both compelled and comforted regarding this God-Man we've chosen to serve. But of all the questions we'd find in the rundown, I have a feeling our favorite would be the one we started with: Question 1.

"What is the chief end of man?" it reads, to which the answer says, "Man's chief end is to glorify God, and to enjoy Him for ever."[5] So many people run around in a panic, trying to sort out the purpose of life, when all they need to do is scan the Shorter! Your purpose is to glorify and enjoy God.

The verses that support the Catechism's answer are three: 1 Corinthians 10:31 says, "So, whether you eat or drink, or whatever you do, do all to the glory of God." Romans 11:36 says, "For from him and through him and to him are all things. To him be glory forever. Amen." And Psalm 73:25–28 reads this way:

> Whom have I in heaven but you?
>> And there is nothing on earth that I desire besides you.
> My flesh and my heart may fail,
>> but God is the strength of my heart and my portion
>> forever.
> For behold, those who are far from you shall perish;
>> you put an end to everyone who is unfaithful to you.
> But for me it is good to be near God;
>> I have made the Lord GOD my refuge,
>> that I may tell of all your works.

Did you catch that opening statement from the psalmist? "There is nothing on earth that I desire besides you." On days when you share that testimony, you are most likely in the dead center of God's will for you. Martin Luther said, "Love God, and do what you want."

In fact, there are countless verses from the holy Scriptures that we could include as substantiation for our purpose in life being to glorify and enjoy God, but they all would point to one truth: We can either delight ourselves in our own will and ways or we can delight ourselves in the Lord and his ways. We can't do both simultaneously; to go one way is to forsake the other. It's God or else it's us. The psalmist said in Psalm 37:4, "Delight yourself in the LORD, and he will give you the desires of your heart."

An old hymn says, "Trust and obey, for there's no other way to be happy in Jesus, but to trust and obey."[6] If I lined up the men, women, and students I personally know who would testify to the truth of that chorus, I imagine they would circle the globe. When you choose to put your trust in Jesus instead of in your own ingenuity or professionalism or wit, the stress and strife miraculously melt away. I think this is why we're commanded to delight ourselves in the Lord, as Psalm 37:4 says. God knew that the only way we would be able to carve out a peaceful existence in this broken, fallen world would be to hide ourselves away in him, to *delight* ourselves in him.

We Commit to God

Not long ago, I read an article featuring Drew Brees, the quarterback of the New Orleans Saints, and in it Brees referenced a book that had impacted him deeply and compelled him to give his all, year after year, titled *212: The Extra Degree* and written by Sam Parker and Mac Anderson. The premise of the book is that while water at 211 degrees Fahrenheit is scalding hot, it takes that *one extra degree* to cause the scalding water to boil. "With boiling water comes steam," the authors write. "And steam can power a locomotive."[7]

The idea brought to mind something the angel said to John in his revelation of things to come regarding how "hot" we are to be for Christ. Addressing specifically the church at Laodicea, a body of believers that were known for all the wrong things, the following report came: "I know your works: you are neither cold nor hot. Would that you were either cold or hot! So, because you are lukewarm, and neither hot nor cold, I will spit you out of my mouth" (Revelation 3:15–16).

Had the church been cold, at least it would have been obvious to all that this was not a true people of the "Way." Had the church been hot, so much good could have come through them. The fact that they were lukewarm made them despicable to God. They were saying one thing and doing another. They were preaching a righteous message while continuing to live unrighteous lives. "I will spit you out!" God told them.

He could spit us out as well. A lukewarm life makes God sick. G. Campbell Morgan said that lukewarmness is the worst form of blasphemy.

What God desires is that we would *decide* to commit to him. The Latin etymology of the word *decide* is to kill, to cut off, and in the context of our discussion here, what we're to cut off from our lives is the other gods we're tempted to choose.

We must cut off the god of consumerism.

We must cut off the god of unfaithfulness.

We must cut off the god of selfishness.

We must cut off the god of pride.

Choose *me*, God tells his followers. *Boil over in your fervor for me. Be red-hot in your love for me!*

"Commit your way to the LORD," David writes in Psalm 37:5; "trust in him, and he will act." We are to do the committing, you might have noticed; *God* is the One who acts. In *Surprised by Paradox*, Jen Pollock Michel wrote, "If the kingdom is good news, it surely isn't safe. Because there is no square inch of our lives that Jesus doesn't intend to rule."[8]

As a young man, I made the commitment to give God complete control of my life and my future. "If I was worth Jesus dying for," I reasoned, "then he is worth my living for, in his name." Then and there, I gave my life unconditionally to him. "Lord, fill in the blanks," I prayed. "Wherever you want me to go, whatever you want me to do, whoever you want me to serve, I'm in, no questions asked."

I prayed that prayer while kneeling on a ballfield more than fifty-five years ago, and I haven't regretted it a single day since.

When we surrender our wills to doing his will, he gives us his very best. Some may worry that if they truly surrender their lives to him, he will somehow suck all the joy from their lives. "He'll send me to the back side of nowhere!" the thinking goes. "I'll be miserable for the rest of my life!"

But the apostle Paul says a far different outcome will unfold. "I appeal to you therefore, brothers, by the mercies of God, to present your bodies as a living sacrifice, holy and acceptable to God, which is your spiritual worship," he writes in Romans 12:1–2. "Do not be conformed to this world, but be transformed by the renewal of your mind, that by testing you may discern what is the will of God, what is good and acceptable and perfect." You can trust God unconditionally and say with the psalmist, "I delight to do your will."

In Jeremiah 18, we find a riveting story on how our heavenly Father perfectly makes and shapes our lives: the Parable of the Potter.

By way of context, the prophet Jeremiah was the son of a priest and likely raised as a priest himself in the city of Jerusalem. He was in his twenties when he began to prophesy on behalf of God, and his messages, which were written to Jews facing judgment for disobeying God, pointed to one central theme: *turn away from your sin and toward God before it's too late.* God had been patient with his people; remember, nearly a millennium had passed between God covenanting with them by issuing through Moses the Ten Commandments and the Israelites' captivity in Babylon. But it seemed no amount of long-suffering would be enough for this stiff-necked group. Through tears, this man who was often referred to as the "weeping prophet" begged his fellow countrymen to reverse course, even as they tumbled headlong toward disaster and pain.

To the text. In verses 1 through 11, we read the following:

> The word that came to Jeremiah from the LORD: "Arise, and go down to the potter's house, and there I will let you hear my words." So I [Jeremiah] went down to the potter's house, and there he was working at his wheel. And the vessel he was making of clay was spoiled in the potter's hand, and he reworked it into another vessel, as it seemed good to the potter to do.
>
> Then the word of the LORD came to me: "O house of Israel, can I not do with you as this potter has done? declares the LORD. Behold, like the clay in the potter's hand, so are you in my hand, O house of Israel. If at any time I declare concerning a nation or a kingdom, that I will pluck up and break down and destroy it, and if that nation, concerning which I have spoken, turns from its evil, I will relent of the disaster that I intended to do to it. And if at any time I declare concerning a nation or a kingdom that I will build and plant it, and it if does evil in my sight, not listening to my voice, then I will relent of the good that I had intended to do to it. Now, therefore, say to the men of Judah and the inhabitants of Jerusalem: 'Thus says the LORD. Behold, I am shaping disaster against you and devising a plan against you. Return, every one from his evil way, and amend your ways and your deeds.'"

We see in this powerful scene God's *intention* for his people. We aren't merely the "product of conception," as proponents of abortion would assert. We were intentionally knit together in our mothers' wombs by the careful hand of our almighty Creator. We were made in the image of infallible God. We were crafted on purpose for a purpose, which as we've learned is to glorify and enjoy him.

Further, we see God's *invention* regarding his people. Like a potter at the wheel, lump of clay in his hand, God is making something in and through our lives, actively shaping us into the people he designed us to be.

Historians agree that the practice of making pottery, one of the most ancient art forms, dates to around 18,000 BC when humankind still lived in caves. But despite its long history, the process has remained largely unchanged. The potter places a lump of colorless, shapeless clay onto a pottery wheel; he spins the clay until a general form begins to surface and then molds that form by hand until the desired shape takes hold; and the final piece is then heated in a high-temperature kiln to make the work sturdy, able to sustain daily life.

The reason this process ought to matter to us is that God is the Potter referred to, and you and I are that lifeless lump of clay. To be sure, we have little going for us until God gets his hands on us and begins to shape and mold and form. But oh, the magnificent works of art he crafts when we are pliable in his hands.

So we see *intention* and we see *invention*, but there is something more to be seen here. There is also *intervention* as the Potter reshapes what has become misshapen, thereby putting back together the broken vessel in his hands. There was creation at the beginning as God "formed the man of dust from the ground and breathed into his nostrils the breath of life," as Genesis 2:7 attests. And now there is recreation as God commits himself to perfecting that which is committed to him. Our failures are never final when God is at the wheel.

My point is that it takes patience, persistence, and unparalleled expertise to make a masterpiece from dirty gray clay, and yet that is exactly what God promises to do in our lives when we trust him, when we remain steadfastly committed to him. When we echo the words of that old hymn, "Have Thine own way, Lord; have Thine own way."

We Wait on God

A third and final snapshot of a life being lived in God's will is this: You will happily *wait on God*.

My dear friend Gilberto Corredera has headed up our Spanish-speaking ministry, Prestonwood en Español, for a decade now, growing that group from just a handful of folks to two thousand active members representing nineteen countries—and that says nothing of the seven thousand viewers who tune in to Pastor Corredera's weekly service via the *Telemundo Dallas* feed. To see him today, you'd have no clue that his path to vocational ministry wasn't a straightforward one or that his vast leadership gifts weren't always well known.

Gilberto grew up in Cuba with parents who were active in the country's communist party and self-described atheists. But against that strong set of odds, as a teen Gilberto visited a small church one weekend and came to faith in Christ. When he was eighteen, he sensed a distinct call to the ministry; shortly thereafter he completed his training to become an executive with Evangelism Explosion.

Gilberto married. He and his wife, Yani, welcomed two daughters into the world. And then they decided they wanted something out of life that Cuba would not provide: *freedom*. With no job and no real plan, Gilberto landed in North Texas and found his way to our church. "God had promised me that he would use me to preach the gospel," Gilberto says of those early days, even as he was hired at Prestonwood to work in food services. During his dishwashing shifts, he would keep reminding himself of God's promise to him. He would keep believing God.

About a year into Gilberto's tenure with us, our Spanish-speaking ministry stalled out. I think we had about a hundred people attending back then, and while those women and men were incredibly faithful, turnover in leadership meant that they weren't receiving the care and attention they deserved. Providentially, I happened to meet Gilberto during that season at an event held for the school that is part of our church. I remembered loving his gregariousness with the crowd, his optimistic spirit, and his zeal for the Lord. Several days after that encounter, our minister of missions came to meet with me to lay out a plan for our fledgling group, and as soon as I saw that what we needed was a new lead pastor to revive Prestonwood en Español, I said, "I just met someone who would be *perfect* in that role."

The delight that came over Gilberto's face when he was offered the post was unlike anything I'd ever seen before. Why? Because the turn of events was something he could not have orchestrated himself. He knew that his loving heavenly Father had been working behind the scenes the entire time, bringing this unforeseen, unbelievable, and unprecedented situation to pass. I'd be hard-pressed to find another member of our staff who has meant as much to an individual ministry as Gilberto has meant to those he leads. At five foot six, his stature may be slight, but his zest for ministry is *huge*. The Cuban Missile, I call him. For when he takes aim with the gospel, look out! We have the words of Ephesians 3:20–21 engraved on an interior wall at Prestonwood, and whenever I walk by this promise that God is "able to do far more abundantly than all that we ask or think, according to the power at work within us," I can't help but think of Pastor Gilberto Corredera, a faithful man who never stopped believing that God's plan was worth waiting for.

If there is a better definition of God's will than this idea of constantly returning to him—to delight in him, to commit more of ourselves to him, to wait on him—I don't know what it is. The Master Craftsman—God himself—is weaving a beautiful tapestry out of both your life and mine, and if I could give you only one piece of advice regarding any aspect of life, it would be this: Let him work his artistry as he sees fit. "He has made everything beautiful in its time," Solomon writes in Ecclesiastes 3:11.

That beautiful thing can include you.

9

Giving Good Gifts

Run to and fro everywhere, holy fires, beautiful fires; for you are the light of the world, nor are you put under a bushel. He whom you cleave unto is exalted, and has exalted you. Run to and fro, and be known unto all nations.

St. Augustine, *Confessions*

"But you will receive power when the Holy Spirit has come upon you, and you will be my witnesses in Jerusalem and in all Judea and Samaria, and to the end of the earth."

Acts 1:8

Years ago, one of our teaching pastors was thrown a curve ball when, as he opened his Bible onstage to begin his message, the lights flickered, popped, and then totally went out. This was at our north campus where the main gathering space has no exterior walls—and thus no natural light. A few security lights hummed to life, but for all 1,200 people in the room, the contrast was quite a shock. I got the biggest kick out of what happened next.

The pastor reached into his sport-coat pocket, tugged out his phone, flicked on a flashlight app, spread his notes across the podium, and preached his entire sermon in the dark.

All went well until the end of the service when he had a decision to make. Generally, we conclude every service at Prestonwood with an invitation for people who are considering surrendering their lives to Jesus to come forward, meet with a trained spiritual counselor, and have any questions answered that might be lingering in their minds. But to give an altar call in the dark? It had never been done before. Would it be wise to do it now?

He decided the answer was yes.

When the end of the service came, he motored on as if nothing had happened to the building's entire electrical circuitry as person after person, couple after couple, family after family—led by smartphones of their own—rose and made their way forward. They came because they were broken. They came because they were hurting. They came because they were weary of trying to be their own gods and falling short. Twenty-one people gave their lives to Jesus that morning, proving that although the lights were off, God's power still was on.

God's power *always* is on.

The second by-product of a reignited faith is that you simply can't keep the good news to yourself. It's too good to keep to yourself! Of the two types of sacrifices delineated in the Old Testament, only one was used to accomplish redemption for sin. "Propitiatory sacrifices," they were called, sacrifices that involved the sacrifice of animals and the use of their blood to symbolize the covering of sin. Any guesses as to the other sacrifice referenced? It was the sacrifice of celebration, what the writer of Hebrews calls a "sacrifice of praise" (Hebrews 13:15).

Several times a year, the Israelites would gather at feasts and festivals for no other reason than to celebrate God's faithfulness to them over the years. There would be singing and dancing and massive amounts of food. And as the older set shared their remembrances of God's goodness, the next generation listened up. *This is the same God we are following*, they must have thought. *He will be equally good to us!* And in the same way that those believers shared the good news—person to person, heart to heart—we get to share the good news today. We get to participate in a modern-day sacrifice of celebration, a bona fide sacrifice of praise. "Look at how faithful God has been to me!" the message of evangelism declares. "He will be faithful to you too."

For as difficult and complicated as believers have tried to make evangelism over the years, what I've just described is truly all there is to it: When you yourself recognize the unique adequacy of Jesus Christ and then joyously declare that unique adequacy to another, you have officially "evangelized." In John 7, near the end of a festival like the ones we talked about before, this one the Feast of Booths, Jesus said to the celebrants who had gathered, "If anyone thirsts, let him come to me and drink. Whoever believes in me, as the Scripture has said, 'Out of his heart will flow rivers of living water'" (vv. 37–38).

Jesus also used this imagery when speaking with the Samaritan woman he encountered at the well, and the point he was making in both instances is that once a person becomes a "true believer" in the sufficiency of Christ, that person experiences a heart flowing with "rivers of living water." In the same way that you don't have to pump a river to get the water to flow, you don't need to pump your enthusiasm for sharing Jesus with someone who has not yet met him. If you are a faithful follower of Jesus, that river is just going to *flow*.

Certainly, there is a place for developing the "skills" of evangelism—for learning how to begin a spiritual conversation, how to listen well and in a nonjudgmental manner, how to defend the core tenets of our faith, and so on—but as a starting point, we do well to perform this simple assessment:

1. As a follower of Jesus, am I fired up with enthusiasm for him?

2. Am I talking about him to people who don't know him?

3. Is there a sense that the persistent *flow* of my life is both relying on and speaking about the adequacy of Christ?

To read the book of Acts—penned under the inspiration of the Holy Spirit by the apostle and physician Luke—is to find a group of people answering all three of those questions with unfettered yeses. "Repent and be baptized," Peter declared on the Day of Pentecost before the masses, "every one of you in the name of Jesus Christ for the forgiveness of your sins, and you will receive the gift of the Holy Spirit. For the promise is for you and for your children and for all who are far off, everyone whom the Lord our God calls to himself" (Acts 2:38–39).

The text goes on to say that "with many other words he [Peter] bore witness and continued to exhort them, saying, 'Save yourselves from this crooked generation'" (v. 40). And in response to Peter's enthusiastic evangelistic message, "there were added that day about three thousand souls" (v. 41) to those who counted themselves among believers in Christ.

Three thousand confessions of faith in one day after just one sermon was preached.

I think you'd agree that was a very good day, and yet how often do you and I ponder the fact that the very same Spirit at work in Peter that day is at work presently—in us? "But you will receive power when the Holy Spirit has come upon you," Acts 1:8 promises, "and you will be my witnesses in Jerusalem and in all Judea and Samaria, and to the ends of the earth." Reading stories such as this one about three thousand people surrendering their lives to Jesus in one fell swoop takes one's breath away. It inspires us to ask God for that type of revival in the here and now. It reinvigorates our understanding that we are evangelists too and that such outcomes are ours to be had. The reason the Great Commission isn't viewed as our duty as much as our *delight* is that we recognize that there is no greater joy in this earthly existence than to be used to point another person to Christ. When God said to "be his witnesses in the earth," he was inviting us into the greatest adventure imaginable. To say yes to that adventure is to apprehend that Jesus' central mission is to seek and save what is lost and that our central mission is to help him get that done.

Across nearly fifty years of ministry, I've coached tens of thousands of believers on how to view themselves as evangelists, how to behave as evangelists, and how to train up newcomers to the faith to be evangelists as well. And while the content of those conversations could fill many volumes, I'd like to whittle it for you here by offering a few high points to consider. For our purposes in this chapter, let's consider a few groups of four as an evangelism primer of sorts: First, there are four spiritual truths regarding all people; next, there are four gifts you can give through evangelism; and finally, there are four profound effects that unfold in a person's life when evangelistic efforts are Spirit led. Let's look at each in turn.

What's True of Us All

Despite what statisticians might tell you about rising apathy in younger generations for the things of God, I find that people of all ages and from every imaginable background remain interested in spiritual matters for the simple reason that before a person is "in Christ," that person is spiritually empty. This is the first of four truths of all people, everywhere.

We All Start Spiritually Empty

A quote attributed to French mathematician and theologian Blaise Pascal goes like this: "There is a God-shaped vacuum in the heart of every person which cannot be filled by any created thing, but only by God, the Creator." What this means for you and me as evangelists is that we have something that every single person living outside of intimate relationship with God desperately wants and urgently needs. At the root of every other need is this spiritual need, and you and I have the answer to that.

Everyone Is Lonely without God

I know that people who are perpetually surrounded by other people can seem impossibly connected and contented and like they're enjoying about all the community a person could imagine. And yet if that person is not living in close relationship with God through Jesus, then that person is lonely to the core. "Cosmic loneliness," this is called, the sense that regardless of how many people flank me, I am all alone in this world.

God made us for relationship, but human relationships cannot substitute for the fundamental relationship we desire with him.

Everyone Begins Guilty of Sin

The prophet Isaiah wrote in Isaiah 53:6 that "all we like sheep have gone astray; we have turned—every one—to his own way; and the LORD has laid on him the iniquity of us all." That little phrase "every one" includes us all, which means that nobody escapes this life without needing forgiveness for his or her sins. Inside every human heart is a ferocious sense of guilt for the wrongs we have committed against the One who created us and loves us and has distinct purposes for our lives. And while we can try to deny that guilt by insisting we are "good people," or try to ignore that guilt by staying busy, or try to assuage that guilt by racking up good works, or try to medicate that guilt by using and abusing drugs and alcohol and sex, the only effective way to address the reality that we have fallen short of God's standard of perfection is to ask that perfect God for help, which he gladly provides in the person of Christ.

Every soul *cries out* for forgiveness from Jesus until that soul *finds* forgiveness in him.

Fear of Death Is a Very Real Fear

Have you ever noticed that when people refer to the death of a loved one, they try to soften their language so that they don't have to actually say "died"? They will speak of someone "not making it" or "passing away" or—and this is big among believers—"going home to Jesus."

We don't like the idea of death.

We don't like to speak about the idea of death.

We don't like the fact that we're going to face death.

We don't like . . . *death*, even though death runs long in my family, and in yours.

I was talking with a guy once who had a pretty cavalier attitude toward death and was speaking of his own death as though one day he would be living and then *poof*, the lights would be out and the party would be over. But that's not at all how death will occur—at least not for humans, who possess eternal souls. Death will be an end for us, but it will also be a beginning. The question is, What will it be the beginning of—eternal agony or eternal bliss?

In addition to a physical death, which every living person will someday experience, the Bible speaks of an eternal death in which people are marked for eternity spent in the presence of God or eternity spent in hell. I know that hell isn't a popular subject these days, but what Jesus is clear about, I stick close to. And he was *very* clear about hell.

"When the Son of Man comes in his glory," we read in Matthew 25, "and all the angels with him, then he will sit on his glorious throne. Before him will be gathered all the nations, and he will separate people one from another as a shepherd separates the sheep from the goats. And he will place the sheep on his right, but the goats on the left. Then the King will say to those on his right, 'Come, you who are blessed by my Father, inherit the kingdom prepared for you from the foundation of the world'" (vv. 31–34).

Those on Jesus' left receive a message of a far different kind: "Then he will say to those on his left," verse 41 says, "'Depart from me, you cursed, into the eternal fire prepared for the devil and his angels.'"

Again, I take no delight in speaking of the eternal damnation of any human soul. But how else are we to interpret Jesus' words here than to believe that hell is real?

"It is appointed for man to die once," says the writer of Hebrews in chapter 9, verse 27, "and after that comes judgment." We will die physically. We will die *eternally*. Death will eventually come to us all.

This brings us to the third kind of death we need to grasp in our minds if we expect to be effective evangelists in our sphere. The Bible speaks of physical death, it speaks of eternal death, and it speaks of a kind of death that produces each of those: *spiritual death*. The apostle Paul writes in Ephesians 2,

> And you were dead in the trespasses and sins in which you once walked, following the course of this world, following the prince of the power of the air, the spirit that is now at work in the sons of disobedience—among whom we all once lived in the passions of our flesh, carrying out the desires of the body and the mind, and were by nature children of wrath, like the rest of mankind. But God, being rich in mercy, because of the great love with which he loved us, even when we were dead in our trespasses, made us alive together with Christ—by grace you have been saved—and raised us up with him and seated us with him in the heavenly places in Christ Jesus, so that in the coming ages he might show the immeasurable riches of his grace in kindness toward us in Christ Jesus.
>
> vv. 1–7

When he speaks of our being "dead in our trespasses," he is referring to the sort of death that is remedied only by being born again. "Truly, truly, I say to you, unless one is born again he cannot see the kingdom of God," Jesus says to the spiritual seeker Nicodemus in John 3:3. Why must we be born again? Because unless we experience spiritual rebirth, we will die as a result of our sin. "Do you not know that if you present yourselves to anyone as obedient slaves, you are slaves of the one whom you obey, either of sin," Paul writes in Romans 6:16, "which leads to death [spiritual death], or of obedience, which leads to righteousness [spiritual life]?"

Take the kindergartner who is caught pulling a classmate's hair and then kicking that classmate in the shin. The teacher says, "Young lady, how'd the devil get you to do such awful things?" To which the little girl replies, "Well, the devil only put me up to pulling her hair. I thought up the shin kicking on my own." Before we knew Jesus, you and I were just like that little girl. Before Christ, we were controlled by the world's whims and ways as well, walking according to "the course of this world," as Paul said, which of course centers itself on me, me, me. ("Enough about me," said the recovering egotist. "Now, what do *you* think about me?")

We may smile at that little girl's precociousness, but that sin streak she's manifesting, if left unchecked and unresolved by the blood of Jesus, will hamstring her ability in coming years to experience the abundance that is hers in Christ. It's funny until it's not funny, right? This is a little like that. Sin will lead us right to physical death, and physical death that occurs apart from the saving knowledge of Jesus will lead us right to eternal death. This spiritual death is serious business, then. We are wise to tread carefully here. What's more, we are wise to speak boldly on behalf of Christ, the One who has conquered *every last form* of death.

Four Gifts You Can Give

We've established that despite appearances, people who are living outside of a saving relationship with Jesus are empty, lonely, guilty, and afraid, which would be utterly devastating news were it not for what we will talk about next: the four gifts evangelism offers anyone who would come to Christ and live for him.

The Gift of a Renewed Life

In John 9, John recounts the extraordinary occasion of Jesus healing a man born blind. The disciples wondered if the man's blindness was a result of the man's sin, or perhaps the sins of his family, but Jesus had a different take. "It was not that this man sinned, or his parents, but that the works of God might be displayed in him" (v. 3). To the shock of everyone gathered there, Jesus then spat on the ground, made mud with his saliva, anointed the man's eyes with the mud, and told him to go wash in a nearby pool. After the man did as he'd been instructed, he was able to see at last.

As is often the case when we undergo massive changes in life, people have questions. Specifically, the people that day wanted to know how this turn of events could have been possible, and who on earth could accomplish such a miraculous feat, and whether this "great healer" the man spoke of was in fact a sinner or whether he was, as he'd claimed, *from God*. After being peppered for several minutes, the once-blind man said in exasperation, "Whether he [referring to Jesus] is a sinner I do not know. One thing I do know, that though I was blind, now I see" (v. 25).

The religious folks in the bunch cast the man out, believing he was a heretic, but Jesus knew the score. "Do you believe in the Son of Man?" he asked him, to which the man replied, "And who is he, sir, that I may believe in him?" (v. 35). "You have seen him," Jesus told him, "and it is he who is speaking to you" (v. 37).

"Lord, I believe," the man said (v. 38). And then he worshiped him.

Jesus looked at this new believer and said, "For judgment I came into this world, that those who do not see may see, and those who see may become blind" (v. 39).

Conceit and human ingenuity—the belief that we've got this "life" thing down will result in spiritual blindness, but for those who are willing to surrender their ways, for the first time in their lives, *they will see*. In 2 Corinthians 5:17, Paul says, "Therefore, if anyone is in Christ, he is a new creation. The old has passed away; behold, the new has come."

What good news this is for anyone wanting a do-over! If people you know are tired of fighting the same old battles and tired of being stuck in the same old habits and tired of wrestling with the same old sin, they need to know that *new life* is waiting for them. It's never too late for a new beginning.

Out with the old.

In with the new.

This is the promise of Christ.

The Gift of a Robust Faith

A second gift that evangelism gives is a robust faith, a strength that can withstand the storms of life, and as we've discussed, *those storms do come*. Once a person is saved, that person is eternally saved, which means that salvation has been accomplished in his or her heart.

"Truly, truly, I say to you," says John 5:24, "whoever hears my word and believes him who sent me has eternal life. He does not come into judgment, but has passed from death to life." Nothing can strip salvation from a person who is "in Christ." What confidence this affords! No longer do we have to rely on our own ideas, our own direction, our own gut instincts about where to go and what to do; we now have a constant companion in God's

Holy Spirit, who will help us to overcome every tough time. What's more, based on Hebrews 7:25, we know that "He [Jesus] always lives to make intercession for them [his saints]."

Jesus is praying for you.

Jesus is praying for me.

It's wonderful to have friends and family members interceding on our behalf. But to have *Jesus*, praying that we would stay strong in our faith? That is next-level prayer, I'd say.

This robust faith comes from the permanent nature of salvation; from the guidance of the Holy Spirit; from the prayers of Jesus, our Savior; and also from the immutable love of God.

When Deb and I were new parents, we and our son, Jason, who is now in his forties and a father himself, were living in east Fort Worth, serving at Sagamore Hill Baptist Church. Jason was stumbling around on the sidewalk one day, as toddlers do, and so to steady my son, I offered him my hand. He wrapped his fingers around my index finger and did fine for a few steps, but then *pow*, he tripped on a crack in the sidewalk and clapped his chin against the unforgiving concrete. The shriek that emerged from my son's mouth defied his tiny size. *Man*, did that hurt.

Years later, I was studying for a sermon and came across Psalm 37:24 for the umpteenth time. "Though he fall," it reads, "he shall not be utterly cast down; for the Lord upholds him with His hand" (NKJV). I thought back to that episode with Jason and realized that while it's one thing for me to let my son hold on to me, it would have been a different thing altogether if instead I'd held on to him. God holds on to those who are in him, and he never, ever lets go. "He who began a good work in you will bring it to completion at the day of Jesus Christ," Paul writes in Philippians 1:6.

He'll hold me.

He'll hold you.

He will.

The Gift of a Righteous Path

A third gift of evangelism is that of a righteous path, a path marked by devotion in loving God and by selflessness in serving others. Perhaps the greatest joy of my life is knowing that as I stay surrendered to the Lord Jesus, I will be led in the direction that most honors him. I mess up—everyone does—but I don't stay messed up for long, and there is great comfort in that. For the believer, the prompting of the Spirit is toward goodness, toward gentleness, toward peacefulness, toward joy . . . it's toward *all the things* a person wants to be.

In Jesus, our search can be over. We can become what God created us to be.

The Gift of a Relevant Message

Romans 1:16 reminds us that we need not be "ashamed of the gospel of Christ, for it is the power of God to salvation for everyone who believes, for the Jew first and also for the Greek" (NKJV). In other words, this invitation to salvation, which is sorely needed by all, is eager to empower everyone who wishes to say yes.

When a person comes to faith in Christ, he or she is then found in possession of the most relevant message there is: "You are loved by God. You can be forgiven of your sin. You can enjoy the presence of God forever. Confess with your mouth that Jesus is Lord, and believe in your heart that God has raised him from the dead, and you will be saved, today."

"I was sinking deep in sin," the old song goes, "far from that peaceful shore / Very deeply stained within, sinking to rise no more / But the Master of the sea, heard my despairing cry / From the waters lifted me, now safe, safe am I."[1]

Oh, that we would seek him! And compel others to do the same.

Evangelism's Fourfold Effect

We've explored the four truths of humanity, which serve as the reasons people will *always* be open to Christ. We've looked at the four gifts that evangelism offers to those who would surrender their lives to Christ. And now, the fourfold effect of evangelism, which answers the question, *How does a person receive those gifts?*

Throughout Scripture, the idea of evangelism is referred to as "proclamation." For example, in Colossians 1:28, Paul writes, "Him [Jesus] we *proclaim*, warning everyone with all wisdom, that we may present everyone mature in Christ." In Luke 9:1–2, the apostle Luke writes of Jesus, "And he called the twelve together and gave them power and authority over all demons and to cure diseases, and he sent them out to *proclaim* the kingdom of God and to heal."

Even in the Old Testament, the trend holds: "But for this purpose," Moses quotes God as saying, "I have raised you up, to show you my power, so that my name may be *proclaimed* in all the earth" (Exodus 9:16, emphasis added in all three passages).

To proclaim is "to speak something out, to announce, to state," and so, leaning into that usage, we'll refer in this section to the person who is being exposed to the good news of God's grace as the "hearer," even as the first part of the fourfold effect of evangelism requires that you and I largely keep our mouths shut!

The Hearer Is Considered

With so much good news to share, I know it's tempting to steamroll people until they cry for mercy and accept Jesus as Savior already. Let me caution you to fight that temptation every time. The reason that the saying "People don't care how much you know until they know how much you care" is cliché is because it is true. Nobody likes a know-it-all—especially when that know-it-all is a perfect stranger. Before you engage in a spiritual conversation with someone, take time to *consider* who they are. How was it that your path came to cross theirs? What do they do for work, or where do they go to school? Are they close to their family? What are some things they love to do in their spare time?

If the person is someone you already know in passing—a neighbor, perhaps, or a colleague—then consider what dynamics are at play in their life today. How is work (or school) going for them? How are their key relationships? How is their health and the health of their loved ones? What anticipated plans are on the books for them?

If you can't answer questions along these lines regarding the person you're thinking of sharing Christ with, then you're probably not ready to share Christ. To consider another is to accept the hearer into your care, to invite the hearer into conversation with you, to demonstrate respect for the hearer by asking meaningful questions instead of flogging him or her with premature facts.

The Hearer Is Comforted

After you have built a level of rapport with the hearer—and the Holy Spirit prompts you to go on—consider checking to see if you might ask a question that's a little deeper than the depths you've already plumbed. If the hearer is agreeable, then ask something along the lines of, "Has there ever been a spiritual aspect to your life?"

At this point, your job is simply to listen. You don't need to have a spiel running through your mind that you're ready to launch on them. You don't need to be prepping apologetics-style answers to refute any negative thing they say about God, the Church, or Christians in general. You need only to fall silent, pray fervently, and listen well.

Whenever I'm entering into a conversation with another person, I reflect on the Parable of the Prodigal Son and do my best to set my countenance to that of the wayward son's father upon the son's return. Do you remember that part of the story? The son had arrogantly demanded his share of the inheritance before his father had even died and then took off to indulge in a high-flying lifestyle where he blew every last dime on himself. In the end, he found himself eating pig slop and wishing he were as "blessed" as his father's hired hands back home.

Finally at the end of his rope, the son decided to return to his father. And as he came up the path that led to his boyhood home, his father saw who it was. "While he [the son] was still a long way off," Luke 15:20 says, "his father saw him and felt compassion, and ran and embraced him and kissed him."

Seeing intently, treating another with compassion, eagerly showing our affection—this is the posture we must assume.

As you pick your way through the beginnings of spiritual dialogue with another, ask yourself, *Is this person feeling comforted by me?*

The Hearer Is Challenged

This next part is key. In an anything-goes society, we must be careful to stick to the truth. It is critical to consider the hearer and to comfort the hearer, but be sure you don't stop there! Also *challenge* the hearer to confront Jesus, to confront the Scriptures, to confront Christianity as a whole. "No matter what we currently believe, we must all confront Christianity," writes Rebecca McLaughlin in her wise work *Confronting Christianity*, "the most widespread belief system in the world, with the most far-reaching intellectual footprint, and a wealth of counterintuitive wisdom concerning how humans should thrive."[2]

If you've ever formally studied the art of evangelism—either by taking a training course such as Evangelism Explosion or by reading up on the subject—then you know that a common practice in challenging hearers is to ask two diagnostic questions of them: First, "If you were to die today, do you know beyond the shadow of a doubt that you would go to heaven?" And second, "If you were to stand before Jesus today, and he were to ask why he should let you into heaven, what would you say?"

Innumerable teams of budding evangelists from our church have scoured the Dallas–Fort Worth metroplex, going to strip malls and supermarkets and cafés with those two questions on their lips. And you can't imagine the fascinating conversations they've happened upon. I'm telling you: *People are interested in spiritual things.*

In response to these questions, three themes emerge: People say they *think* they're going to heaven and that Jesus will let them in, because they've been a "pretty good person most of the time" (or some such thing); they say they are fairly certain they're *not* going to heaven, because they're pretty mischievous most of the time; or they say that yes, absolutely they will go to heaven, because they've surrendered their life to Christ. Unless you're talking to someone who is adamantly in denial that heaven exists, or is already living in intimate fellowship with the Father by way of a saving relationship with Jesus Christ, then it behooves both you and the hearer to explain a bit about grace. You might say, "Would you be open to hearing about how I came to know that I am for sure going to heaven and that Jesus will for sure let me in once I arrive?"

At this point in the conversation, you will need to have something to say! There are plenty of evangelism-training programs you might avail yourself of. You might choose to memorize the various Bible verses that make up the tool known as the Roman Road. You might ask God to point you to the Scriptures he would have you cite that explain big-ticket subjects such as how a person comes into relationship with him. You might get your hands on an EvangeCube, a Rubik's Cube–looking block that covers the entire gospel presentation in six flips of its sides, which was codesigned by my longtime friend Nathan Sheets. Whatever you do, be sure to help the hearer understand the core aspects of our faith, including the following:

1. All people have sinned and are thus separated from God.
2. God loved us enough to send his Son, Jesus, to die on a cross as a sacrifice for our sin.

3. Three days after Jesus was crucified, God raised him from the dead. Today, Jesus sits at God's right hand, having completed the work God asked him to do.

4. The Bible says that Jesus is the only way for us to be reconciled to God and enjoy fellowship with him again.

5. We also know from Scripture that at the time of Jesus' return to the earth, we each will have to give an account for our lives and will face heaven or hell based on whether we trusted in Christ.

6. Receiving Jesus as Savior means confessing with our mouth that Jesus is Lord and believing in our heart that God raised him from the dead.

Remember, in all things, exhibit the love of Christ, being careful to challenge the hearer to contemplate Jesus. You're not challenging the hearer to a duel.

Love and grace.

Love and grace.

Love and grace.

At all times, love and grace.

The Hearer Is Compelled

In his writings to the church at Corinth, the apostle Paul said, "Behold, now is the favorable time; behold, now is the day of salvation" (2 Corinthians 6:2). Which means that if the person you are talking with is considering surrendering his or her life to Jesus, encourage that person to act on that impulse today. Nobody is guaranteed a tomorrow; all we have is this very breath.

Not long ago, on a Saturday night, a man in his mid-thirties attended service at Prestonwood. After the service ended, he remained in his seat, head in his hands, shoulders shaking as he uncontrollably wept. An older man named John, who has been around our church since its inception, happened to notice the young man and quietly, gently approached him. "Is there anything I can do to help you?" John asked him, to which he said through choked syllables, "I've never been in a church before. This is my first time."

"I've never heard the things that were said tonight," he continued. "I never knew about God's grace, and about the forgiveness of Christ, and about how *easy* it is to become a follower of his."

"Those who seek me find me," Jesus promises in Proverbs 8:17 (NIV).

How deeply satisfying it is when we can aid them in that search.

10

And So, We Begin Again

The way to heaven is ascending; we must be content to travel up hill, though it be hard and tiresome, and contrary to the natural bias of our flesh.

Jonathan Edwards, *The Christian Pilgrim*

Therefore lift your drooping hands and strengthen your weak knees, and make straight paths for your feet, so that what is lame may not be put out of joint but rather be healed. Strive for peace with everyone, and for the holiness without which no one will see the Lord.

Hebrews 12:12–14

It is said that only two of the seven million dollars in damages sustained at Thomas Edison's vast West Orange, New Jersey, laboratory, during the fire that consumed the entire complex, was covered by insurance. The lab, which had replaced his famed Menlo Park outfit, contained his records, his patents, his inventions, and more. The tangible aspects of his life's work had gone up in smoke that afternoon in December 1914, and yet as he and his wife watched firefighters unsuccessfully battle the blaze for hours, the great inventor had but one thing to say: "Although I am over sixty-seven years old, I'll start all over again tomorrow."

And that's exactly what he did.

"Cleanup work at the devastated site began the next day when all 7,000 employees reported for duty," wrote one New Jersey historian. "Reconstruction plans quickly followed."[1] Hundreds of the more than 1,000 patents issued to Edison were applied for *after* that terrible fire.

That is perseverance—the third by-product of a reignited faith.

For the believer, the persevering posture sounds a lot like Mr. Edison's response to that fire: "Tomorrow, we start all over again."

Regardless of what has tripped us up, we can always begin again.

In Hebrews 12, the writer exhorts us as believers to consider Jesus "who endured from sinners such hostility against himself, so that you may not grow weary or fainthearted" (v. 3). Later in the passage, he adds more texture to the counsel still: "Therefore lift your drooping hands and strengthen your weak knees," he writes in verses 12–16, "and make straight paths for your feet, so that what is lame may not be put out of joint but rather be healed. Strive for peace with everyone, and for the holiness without which no one will see the Lord. See to it that no one fails to obtain the grace of God; that no 'root of bitterness' springs up and causes trouble, and by it many become defiled; that no one is sexually immoral or unholy like Esau, who sold his birthright for a single meal."

What we have here is a litany of reasons for which we tend not to be able to persevere in the faith; would you agree? We get tired. We get distracted. We grow bitter. We forget what holiness demands of us. We fall into a terrible depression for twelve months straight and believe down to our toes that we'll never, ever find our way out. As a result, we are "put out of joint," as the writer of Hebrews puts it. Or, leaning into a metaphor the apostle Paul is fond of, we let ourselves get sidelined from the race we're supposed to be running.

In 1 Corinthians 9:24, he writes, "Do you not know that in a race all the runners run, but only one receives the prize? So run that you may obtain it." Earlier in the passage we were looking at in Hebrews 12, we are told to "run with endurance the race that is set before us" (v. 1). Incidentally, this is one of the reasons I've always believed the book of Hebrews to have been written by Paul, as the imagery of the runner running a race is distinctive, showing up in just those two spots. Either way, may we grasp the metaphor at hand, which is that there is a race that as followers of Jesus we are competitors (not just participants) in, and the organizer of this race—God himself—trusts that we're running to *win*.

Made—and **Remade**—Brand-New

In my neck of the woods in north Texas, any car collector worth his or her whitewalls and wire wheels knows the name Amos Minter. Amos, who is a longtime member of Prestonwood, has been running Minter Thunderbirds for more than fifty years now, and he has a restoration facility that's nearly an acre in size. He has sold restored 1955, 1956, and 1957 Ford T-Birds to more people with household names than he can count, which tells you the level of restoration work he does. He works on cars that you and I would consider vehicular disasters—they're broken down, horribly discolored, and rusted out—and yet in Amos's eyes they're *gold*. He sees where the project is headed, and he's eager to stay the course.

In a manner of speaking, this is how God views you and me. Even as our outward bodies are perishing—and if you're around my age, you *know* that's the truth—our inner person can be renewed each day we're alive. God commits himself to renewing us, just like Amos renews those old cars. God sees where the project is headed with us and says, "Hang on. Things are gonna get *good*."

As you and I are faithful to uphold his Word and stay connected to him in prayer and engage wholeheartedly with the Bride of Christ, the Church, as we persist in laying down our doubts, discontentment, and distress and picking up faith, gratitude, and peace instead, we become the people he envisions, people who embody and typify his Son. To take a broken-down, beat-up life and transform it by his Spirit into an eternal collector's item, so to speak, surely gives him the greatest thrill. He just *knew* we would turn out well. He just *knew* his work would pay off.

If you're like me, then you can recount plenty of times when persevering through tough stuff served you well. The people I know who really know their way around a gym tell me that what I experienced is true for almost everyone: Right when you're about to give up on a new diet-and-exercise plan, the body gives in and shifts. Weight comes off in a hurry. Mass moves itself around. Energy runs right through the roof. Ten years fly off your face. The reason most people don't experience those radical changes is because they give up before the shifts occur. To experience the blessings of perseverance, remember, we've got to persevere.

The same holds true for finances: If you sock away a few dollars from each paycheck, it will feel like drops in a bucket for quite some time, until the day comes that you say, "I've got some real money in there now." The blessings of perseverance come to those who persevere.

Or what about marriage? With the divorce rate still hovering at 50 percent, I suspect that at least a portion of those marriages that split up would have been well served by slowing their pace, taking their foot off the gas pedal, and persevering a day, a week, a month longer. Why? So that they could've seen what blessings of perseverance might come their way, if only they persevered.

This is also true in our occupational worlds. One of the greatest joys of my work life is that I am doing ministry with the same women and men I was doing ministry with thirty-plus years ago.

Isn't that incredible? With all the opportunities that have come their way, they have persevered with me at our church, at times weathering storms, enduring droughts, and rowing for what felt like forever against the wind. But ask them if they're glad they stayed, and to a person they'll say yes. I know because I've done it. They're glad because the perseverance they've manifested has handed them blessings that only persevering people receive.

So if in our natural world we see the benefits of persevering, how much more beneficial might it be to persevere in the supernatural aspects of our lives? The beloved Romans 8:28 promises that "for those who love God all things work together for good, for those who are called according to his purpose." Thanks be to God, we're not finished products. Day by day, we're getting better, and we have God to thank for that. And while you and I might not be able to see the good work that is being done in and through us, our heavenly Father has a grand scheme in mind, which is why he asks us to persevere. *I'm up to something amazing here*, he promises us, *if only you'll stay the course.*

When I've been at my lowest points, that counsel from Hebrews 12 has raised my sights. Let's look back at those words and see what wisdom we can glean in hopes of learning how to never give up on God.

Hands Up, Stand Up, Look Up

I grew up playing ball and have loved sports my entire life. If you've played and watched as much sports as I have, then you know that the first thing to happen when a player gets winded is that his or her hands fall to their sides. If a lineman is gassed, he'll drop his hands to the field until the quarterback is ready to go. If a forward has been sprinting for sixty seconds straight up and down the court and up the court again, then her hands will reach for her knees as she tries to catch her breath. When a distance runner finally crosses the finish line, his hands fall to the track.

The hands are always the first to go; our hands betray the energy we feel. Which is why that opening phrase in Hebrews 12:12 is so powerful: "Therefore lift your drooping hands," it says. *Hands up! Hands up! Hands up!*

I love that imagery because so often when we force our bodies to do something, our brains have no choice but to follow. "Psychologists experimenting with what has come to be known as embodied cognition," one contributor to *Psychology Today* writes, "have long known that facial gestures, in addition to reflecting, can actually influence and alter emotional states."[2] Which means, in a rather fake-it-till-you-make-it paradigm, if you want to feel better, for starters simply *act* like you feel better. On some occasions this actually helps.

How do we persevere when the only reasonable option is to quit? *Hands up!* And then stand up too: "and strengthen your weak knees," verse 12 continues.

The last thing I want to do is limp or lag up to heaven's gate. No, I want to finish with a flourish. I want to race toward my Savior, hands in the air, on knees that are not feeble but *strong*.

Hands up! Even when you're downcast. Even when you're tired.

Stand up! Even when your bed is beckoning, "Just hit snooze again . . . no one will know."

And finally, *look up!*

I'm telling you, anytime you have trouble persevering in life, simply look up and remember Christ, the author and finisher of our faith. I know this life is burdensome. I know that times get tough. But what have you and I faced that Jesus himself did not both encounter and overcome? "We do not have a high priest who is unable to sympathize with our weaknesses," Hebrews 4:15 reports, "but one who in every respect has been tempted as we are, yet without sin." Jesus has been where we are. Jesus has felt the pain that we feel. Jesus has himself been broken by this world's brokenness. And yet Jesus *persevered until the end.*

Steady On

The next phrase in Hebrews 12 says this: "make straight paths for your feet." I've always loved the old Irish blessing, "May the road rise up to meet you. May the wind be always at your back. May the sun shine warm upon your face; the rains fall soft upon your fields and until we meet again, may God hold you in the palm of His hand." I know that on some days, it absolutely will feel like the way forward is socked in by fog, the wind is charging us, and the rain is angrily pelting our face. I've had days like that, and so have you. But what remains true is that the path of righteousness is forever available to those who've surrendered their lives to Christ. This path "is like the light of dawn," Solomon writes in Proverbs 4:18, "which shines brighter and brighter until full day." Which means that as you and I search for that path, we are assured that we will find it. God *always* will make his path known.

I tell you this because the easy part of perseverance is raising our hands, standing to our feet, and looking to God. The hard part? It's *running the race*.

Run God's Race

As we think about what it means to persevere in the faith, let's first remind ourselves that it is *God's race* we are to run.

To read the Bible is to find story after story of reluctant prophets who weren't exactly thrilled to do what God had asked them to do. Moses comes to mind. God asked him to help free the Hebrew people from Egyptian slavery, even as Moses was just sure that someone without a stutter would be better suited for the job.

God asked Jonah to deliver a message to the Ninevites regarding God's everlasting compassion for them, if only they would repent of their sin. But it took a three-day stay in the belly of a fish to convince Jonah that, yes, he *was* the man for the job.

Jeremiah thought he was too young. Gideon thought he was too weak. Paul thought he was too beleaguered by sin. On and on it goes. And yet it is clear that God really does intend to use his followers to accomplish his work in the world. He really does expect that it will be his race, not ours, that we run. "Let us run with endurance the race that is set before us," reads Hebrews 12:1. It is God who sets the race, and it is we who run it; he's the sole sponsor here.

Run God's Race Straight

To persevere, we run God's race, and we run that race *straight*. Go back to Hebrews 12 and you'll see this instruction made plain: "Make straight paths for your feet," it reads, "so that what is lame may not be put out of joint but rather be healed" (v. 13). This is a critical reminder, because yes, while it is God who sets the race before us, we must decide whether we'll stay on the course. If you've got any meaningful amount of life on you, then you've surely taken your fair share of zigs and zags from the main path God would have you on. I know I have. I've wound up on more dead ends than I care to count, pushing and kicking and screaming against the wisdom of Proverbs 4:26, which says, "Ponder the path of your feet."

It's so much easier to just run our hearts out, isn't it, than to *ponder the path of our feet*?

And yet the one who is persevering in God's race knows that God has asked us to run that race straight. "Running straight," according to our passage in Hebrews 12, means first prizing peace. "Strive for peace with everyone," verse 14 tells us—and with everything, I might add. It wasn't until I soulfully sought peace with my depression that I was divinely equipped to pull through.

We just spent an entire chapter on peace, so I won't belabor the subject here. But as it relates to the matter of perseverance, I will say that the primary reason I see believers sidelined from the race God has called them to run, incapable of achieving the peace that is promised to *every* believer of his, is bitterness. Those believers just can't let go of the thing that someone in their past said or did.

It has been said that bitterness is an acid that will destroy its own container. I don't want to be that container; do you? I know that there are real hurts sustained by real people . . . unimaginable hurts, inexcusable hurts, hurts that spin our heads and break our hearts. But to hang on to bitterness is to try to run forward while looking backward. It's nearly impossible to do. My friend Jon Gordon likes to say, "Stop looking backwards. Your life isn't there anymore. It's HERE. Right NOW."[3]

The same spirit of forgiveness that came over Jesus as he was spat on and nailed to a tree can come over us in our time of disillusionment: *"Father, forgive them, for they know not what they do."*

Giving up my right to hurt you for hurting me—that's what forgiveness is. That's what it means to "strive for peace." We *push* until peace rests on us.

Strive for peace with everyone "and for the holiness without which no one will see the Lord," verse 14 continues. We are to strive for peace. And we are to strive for purity. Do you know how many problems would be solved in our world if everyone earnestly strived for those two things in the name of God?

All of them.

Holiness is the beauty of Jesus in us, quite literally *God in us.* Have you ever been in the presence of someone who recently had been in the presence of God? Think of Moses descending Mount Sinai after receiving the second set of tablets on which God had etched the Law; someone like that tends to glow with the radiance of God. This type of divine shine is something no beauty product can achieve; rather, it's an inner light emerging. It's purity, in human form.

Recently, I've been working to memorize a passage in 1 Timothy 6 in which the apostle Paul coaches his protégé Timothy regarding keeping his ways pure. Paul rattles off a laundry list of things to avoid—conceit, unhealthy cravings for controversy and quarrels about words, envy, dissension, slander, constant friction, the love of money, and more—and then says, "But as for you, O man of God, flee these things" (v. 11).

Keep your path straight, Timothy, Paul urges the young man. *Run in the right direction for all your days.*

Then, in case Timothy (or we) needed further clarification on what a life of purity might entail, Paul laid it out in terms that everyone could understand: "Pursue righteousness, godliness, faith, love, steadfastness, gentleness. Fight the good fight of the faith. Take hold of the eternal life to which you were called and about which you made the good confession in the presence of many witnesses" (vv. 11–12).

This counsel begs the question, What are we pursuing today? *To pursue* is to intentionally chase after, to work to attain, to strive for. I wonder, what is it that you pursue?

Later in Hebrews 12, the writer says that believers are to see to it "that no one is sexually immoral or unholy like Esau, who sold his birthright for a single meal" (v. 16). The reference is to the book of Genesis when Esau gave his brother, Jacob, his birthright in exchange for a bowl of stew. His belly was more important than his blessing . . . can you relate at all to that?

Sin takes us farther than we ever wanted to go and keeps us there longer than we ever wanted to stay. Our cravings can get the better of us if we're not careful, which is why the exhortation is so critical to run—to *always* run—straight.

Run God's Race, Straight, for God

If I could add one final build to this concept of staying steady in the spiritual race of life, it would be to run God's race, straight, *for God*. It may seem redundant to exhort us to run for God when we've already acknowledged that it's his race we're running. It's not, and here's why: We can do all the right things for all the wrong reasons and in doing so miss the point of life.

When I was growing up, my dad was everything to me. He wasn't a preacher or a professional athlete. He wasn't an executive or a household name. He was a simple, plainspoken, Arkansan small-business owner who sold corn dogs, and yet to me he hung the moon.

Dad taught me how to play baseball and even sponsored my first team in the Buddy League for six-year-olds. We were the Dan-Dee-Dog Cardinals. I was so proud. Later, when I reached high school, both the quantity and (thankfully) the quality of the games improved, and Dad was there in the bleachers for every single one. I loved my dad. I loved baseball. And I loved God. Those three things equated to a life I loved, but the summer between my sophomore and junior years of college, all three would be shaken. I'd have to work to claw my way back.

That summer was the summer my dad died after suffering a brutal attack by a thief. I've written substantially in other places about how difficult it was for me to put the broken pieces of my heart back together and sort out a way to move ahead. Those were long, arduous days and months that I knew would mark me for the rest of my life.

The winds of change were blowing on the baseball front as well. I had fallen in love, and Deb and I were married that summer. Besides my being wonderfully distracted by my beautiful new bride, I also had come to the realization that barring a miracle, I'd never make it in the big leagues. I'd had a few rifts with my coach and was frustrated, physically tired, and mentally spent. Toward the end of that sophomore season, with only three games on the schedule to play, that coach said something that hit me wrong, and I said, "I'm done. I'm not coming back!"

I walked off the field at the end of that game feeling both absolved and irritated—the latter of the two because of my dad's voice in my head. "*What you start, you finish,*" he would tell me. "*You can choose to stop doing something once you complete your commitment, but don't quit midstream, Jack. Be a man of your word.*"

There in our tiny student-housing residence, I would tell Deb of my inner wrestling match: I was sick of playing, but I'd given my word. Had I acted foolishly by walking away? I thought of the countless hours my dad had poured into my baseball career, I pictured him sitting on the bleachers hollering out his support, I sat with his wisdom regarding being sure never to quit, and I knew what I had to do. With cap in hand, I went to the coach's office one day, I bowed my head, and I said, "Coach, I'm really sorry for walking off. I did the wrong thing. I made the wrong call. That was foolish of me, and I'm sorry. Please, will you forgive me?"

I told my coach that if he'd have me back, I would gladly return, but if he thought it best that I sat out, I'd do so with a joyful heart. It didn't hurt that I was the best hitter on the team, but still, I attribute his warm re-acceptance of me to his making a really classy move that day.

I went back to baseball, but I went back a changed man. Instead of playing for my batting average, or for my coach's approval, or even for the sake of my team, I played those last two years for my dad—for Tom Graham, who watched every game from bleachers in heaven, hollering out his endless encouragement, "Go, Jack, go!"

In Hebrews 12, Jesus is referred to as the "author and finisher of our faith" (v. 2 NKJV). And I like to think that as we are running our race, we are looking to him, not just as the one who initially sets our course but as the one who completes it as well.

We run God's race.

We run God's race, straight.

We run God's race, straight, for God.

Running Through

The central question of perseverance is not in deciding to run, or even in running the race itself, but rather in running through to the finish line—staying the course until the end.

These days, I'm the guy sitting on the bleachers at baseball games, hollering encouragement for my baller grandchildren—four-year-old twins and also little Piper, who started T-ball this year. And one of my favorite moments in any game I watch is when one of those tots gets a hit and starts running. The whole home-team crowd goes nuts. The child reflexively drops the bat and takes off like a lightning bolt toward first base, but then upon arriving at first, the same thing happens every time—that kid jumps onto the base with both feet as if to say, "Yessss. I made it!"

Meanwhile, the coach is going ballistic: "Keep going, keep going, don't stop!" What the runner has failed to realize is that because the defense can't seem to get the ball into the glove, the play is still active. "Run through the base! Run *through*!" the coach will holler, reminding the stunned child how baseball—and also life—works.

I was amused to learn that one of the first lessons Piper received at T-ball was to drop her bat after she connected with a pitch before she started running toward first base. Seems obvious to us all-knowing adults, doesn't it, that you don't want to be weighed down by unnecessary baggage while trying to run like the wind? And yet how many of us wise ones trudge through life heavily burdened, having neglected to drop our bats? "Let us also lay aside every weight, and sin which clings so closely," Hebrews 12:1 says, regarding how to run fast, run well, run *through*.

The next time you're in an airport with some time on your hands, take a look at how many people are running to get to their gates with pounds and pounds of baggage in tow. They've got an across-the-body carry-on bouncing on their hip, a bulging computer bag in one hand, the handle of a roller bag in the other, and a Starbucks cup—filled to the brim with scalding-hot coffee, mind you—balanced precariously in the crook of their arm. I'm no running expert, but to me, those folks always look a little less than smooth. Their gait is awkward, their pace stuttered, their focus interrupted, and as a result, their efficiency is nil. How much better would they be able to run if only they'd lay down all that baggage!

How much better *we'd* be able to run in life if only we would do the same.

One of the more interesting aspects of this "safer at home" season our world has been in for months and months is a certain stripping away of the things that kept us busy day by day. First, the schools were shut down, which meant that kids were home all day, every day, which meant that parents were suddenly homeschool teachers. Next, churches went virtual, which meant that many of the (worthwhile and wonderful) ministry obligations we held were erased from our calendars in a flash. Businesses locked their doors. Restaurants were shuttered. Libraries posted *Sorry, we're closed* signs. Doctors' offices switched to "emergency procedure only" status. Shopping malls, theme parks, college campuses, movie theaters, and beaches looked like ghost towns. And while these shifts have certainly been tumultuous—even traumatic—for plenty of people, another more positive effect has emerged. Collectively, we've seen what life is like sans the distractions, what it feels like to "drop the bat," as it were.

For many believers, these months have afforded them a time of reconnection with the God who set their race to begin with. "How did I get so far off course?" they've asked me. "How did I lose my way?"

"I get it!" I always say to them. "This world can weigh a person down!"

"But given that revival begins in a singular human heart," I continue, "maybe God is on the move through you."

So, I'm not buying this gloom and doom. The best days are still ahead!

The end of that passage in Hebrews 12 tells us that we're headed not for a gloom-and-doom existence, but rather to a *party*, an outright feast. "But you have come to Mount Zion and to the city of the living God," the writer says in verses 22 through 24, "the heavenly Jerusalem, and to innumerable angels in festal gathering, and to the assembly of the firstborn who are enrolled in heaven, and to God, the judge of all, and to the spirits of the righteous made perfect, and to Jesus, the mediator of a new covenant, and to the sprinkled blood that speaks a better word than the blood of Abel."

We persevere because we understand that even the best that this world has to offer will crumble to dust someday, even as we who are eternally knitted to God's heart will remain, be remade, and rise. "Don't love the world's ways. Don't love the world's goods. Love of the world squeezes out love for the Father," John writes in 1 John 2:15–17. "Practically everything that goes on in the world—wanting your own way, wanting everything for yourself, wanting to appear important—has nothing to do with the Father. It just isolates you from him. The world and all its wanting, wanting, wanting is on the way out—but whoever does what God wants is set for eternity" (MSG).

What John is saying in short? *Drop the bat.*

Drop the bat of distraction so that you can run free.

Drop the comparison.

Drop the harsh judgments.

Drop the technology addiction.

Drop the regret.

Drop the mindless pursuit of acquisition.

Drop the busyness that sucks the life right out of you.

Drop the quest for notoriety.

Drop the desire for likes and more likes.

Drop anything that takes your eyes off Jesus, the founder and finisher of our faith.

Drop the bat so that you can run—run steady, run straight, and run through.

In the AD 300s, a child was born to Roman parents living in Britain, Calpurnius and Conchessa. They named the boy Maewyn Succat and loved the child with all their heart. Which is why it was so tragic when he was kidnapped as a teenager and sold into slavery in Ireland, forced to tend to his master's sheep. Maewyn had every reason to grow bitter and cold, to believe that life was a joke at best. But he chose instead to view his six-year captivity differently, believing that God must have a plan for him.

"And so, I begin again," he must have said as he took in this new world.

While roaming the hills of Ireland, Maewyn became fluent both in the Irish language and in the language of prayer. Upon his release, he studied to become a priest and began receiving visions from God. He had moved to France for his studies, and in one recurring vision the people of Ireland were calling him back. "Walk with us once more," the people cried in Maewyn's dreams. "Walk with us once more."

And so the moment God told Maewyn to head back to Ireland, the young priest agreed to go. Returning to the very people who'd held him captive may have seemed to some an ironic move, but to Maewyn—whose priestly name was Saint Patrick—there was no other move to make. He was running the race God had set before him, and he was determined to faithfully run through.

For decades, St. Patrick preached the gospel throughout Ireland, eventually converting the entire *nation* to Christ. Churches were established all over the countryside, and what had been a spiritually stale set of surroundings now popped and crackled to life. During his decades of ministry, Patrick would pen scores of poems and prayers, but one of my favorites has to be his magnificent "Deer's Cry."[4]

"I arise today," the prayer begins, "through the strength of heaven; Light of the sun, Splendor of fire, Speed of lightning, Swiftness of the wind, Depth of the sea, Stability of the earth, Firmness of the rock." It continues:

I arise today
Through God's strength to pilot me;
God's might to uphold me,
God's wisdom to guide me,
God's eye to look before me,
God's ear to hear me,
God's word to speak for me,
God's hand to guard me,
God's way to lie before me,
God's shield to protect me,
God's hosts to save me
Afar and anear,
Alone or in a multitude.

Christ shield me today
Against wounding
Christ with me, Christ before me, Christ behind me,
Christ in me, Christ beneath me, Christ above me,
Christ on my right, Christ on my left,
Christ when I lie down, Christ when I sit down,
Christ in the heart of everyone who thinks of me,
Christ in the mouth of everyone who speaks of me,
Christ in the eye that sees me,
Christ in the ear that hears me.

I arise today
Through the mighty strength
Of the Lord of creation.

We arise today, fellow follower of Jesus, arms held high, steady on sturdy knees, eyes fixed on heaven. We persevere, knowing that the good God who has set our course will sustain us until the end.

Christ accompanying us.

Christ emboldening us.

Christ at the finish line, smiling and saying, *"Well done!"*

11

Gaze Set on Things Unseen

There have been times when I think we do not desire heaven; but more often I find myself wondering whether, in our heart of hearts, we have ever desired anything else.

C. S. Lewis, *The Problem of Pain*

If then you have been raised with Christ, seek the things that are above, where Christ is, seated at the right hand of God. Set your minds on things that are above, not on things that are on earth. For you have died, and your life is hidden with Christ in God. When Christ who is your life appears, then you also will appear with him in glory.

Colossians 3:1–4

If I had to boil down the reignited spiritual life to one key truth, it would be this: Heaven is all around us, and when we have eyes to see it, we can live in its reality now. The journey we have been on to recapture fundamental spiritual practices, to choose to make God-honoring exchanges day by day, has been to bring us to this place of reckoning—by our attitudes, actions, and alliances, will you and I help usher heaven into earth today, or will we further this broken world's agenda, which centers on destruction, disease, and despair? I have yet to meet an earnest believer who hopes for the latter of those two; we want the heavenly option! We want our lives to matter for good.

Let's look, then, at this fourth beautiful by-product of a faith that has been reignited for God. Such faith compels a person to lovingly long for God's will instead of their own. Such faith compels a person to share the good news of the gospel with those living apart from Christ. Such faith compels a person to run the race set before them with all diligence. And finally, such faith *compels a person to long for heaven, their one, true home—eternity spent in the presence of God.*

Heaven: What It Is and How to Get There

As I mentioned, years ago, I was so intrigued by thoughts of the supernatural—the afterlife, eternity, angels, and more—that I wrote an entire book on the topic.[1] And one of the most marvelous truths I was reminded of during my research for that project was that heaven is much closer than we think. It's tempting to see heaven as "out there" somewhere, in a galaxy far, far away, to consider heaven as about as relevant to us earthly beings as the far side of the moon. In reality, though, heaven is near us, all around us, moving among us, close at hand.

During Jesus' earthly ministry, he was asked by a group of Pharisees—the religious leaders of the day—about heaven. When could they expect this "kingdom of God" Jesus so often spoke of to arrive? To which Jesus said, "The kingdom of God is not coming in ways that can be observed, nor will they say, 'Look, here it is!' or 'There!' for behold, the kingdom of God is in the midst of you" (Luke 17:20–21). Indeed, the things of heaven—the onlooking presence of saints, the dutiful servanthood of angels, the eternal presence of our loving Father—have already come to earth . . . and are coming to earth . . . and someday will be here in full. The question is whether you and I have eyes to see it, whether our minds are prepared to take it all in.

Heaven Is Unseen People

In the last chapter, we looked closely at the exhortations in Hebrews 12 regarding our effectively running the race God has set before us, and I want to revisit that passage to address the context here. Prior to the writer's encouragement to "lay aside every weight" and "run with endurance" and look to Jesus, the "founder and perfecter of our faith" (vv. 1–2), we read these words: "Therefore, since we are surrounded by so great a cloud of witnesses" (v. 1). The impact of these words is not to be missed: Along with being surrounded by God's angelic host, onlookers of our earthly existence also include faithful saints who have gone ahead.

You've likely heard that whenever you encounter a "therefore" in Scripture, it's wise to pause and ask what it's *there for*. In this case, the "therefore" at the beginning of Hebrews 12 hearkens back to Hebrews 11. And what we find in Hebrews 11 is a litany of those who lived their lives faithful to God. "By faith Abel offered to God a more acceptable sacrifice than Cain," verse 4 says. "By faith Enoch was taken up so that he should not see death," reads verse 5. On and on it goes:

- By faith Noah constructed an ark—verse 7.
- By faith Abraham went out, not knowing where he was going—verse 8.
- By faith Sarah received power to conceive—verse 11.
- By faith Abraham offered up Isaac—verse 17.
- By faith Isaac invoked future blessings on his sons—verse 20.
- By faith Jacob blessed the sons of Joseph—verse 21.

- By faith Joseph acknowledged the exodus of the Israelites—verse 22.
- By faith Moses denounced the fleeting pleasures of sin—verse 25.
- By faith Rahab gave a friendly welcome to the spies—verse 31.

The writer, realizing that to recount all the faithfulness of those named in Scripture would perhaps take him the rest of his life, works to bring his list to a close:

> And what more shall I say? For time would fail me to tell of Gideon, Barak, Samson, Jephthah, of David and Samuel and the prophets—who through faith conquered kingdoms, enforced justice, obtained promises, stopped the mouths of lions, quenched the power of fire, escaped the edge of the sword, were made strong out of weakness, became mighty in war, put foreign armies to flight. Women received back their dead by resurrection. Some were tortured, refusing to accept release, so that they might rise again to a better life. Others suffered mocking and flogging, and even chains and imprisonment. They were stoned, they were sawn in two, they were killed with the sword. They went about in skins of sheep and goats, destitute, afflicted, mistreated—of whom the world was not worthy—wandering about in deserts and mountains, and in dens and caves of the earth.
>
> And all these, though commended through their faith, did not receive what was promised, since God had provided something better for us, that apart from us they should not be made perfect.
>
> vv. 32–40

Then comes the "therefore." And I think you'd agree that anyone who stood as firm as these folks stood—suffering mocking, being flogged, even being martyred for their faith—is someone we want on our side. How heartening it is to realize that as we face trials and tribulations of our own, this "great cloud" indeed surrounds us, helping us take heart, cheering us on.

Whenever I think about that band of witnesses mentioned in the book of Hebrews, my mind chases off to some spiritual heroes of my own. You know that I view my dad in that light, but equally true was that my grandfather was a bona fide hero to me. Sometimes when I preach, I can hear my granddad, who taught me so much of what I know of the Scriptures, saying, "Preach it to 'em, Jackie!"

That always makes me smile. Preach it to 'em, Jackie. Tell 'em the truth about God.

My older brother, thirteen years my senior, is also in heaven, and when I think about how he set my spiritual pace from the youngest of ages, I'm overcome with gratitude that his eye is on me still today.

My dear departed friend and America's onetime foremost motivational speaker Zig Ziglar passed away nearly a decade ago, and yet so often I all but audibly hear his voice in my head, pressing me onward with wisdom and wit: "Every choice you make has an end result."[2] "Happiness is not pleasure. It is victory."[3] Or the well-known quip, "People say motivation doesn't last, to which I say, 'Neither does bathing, which is why we recommend doing it daily.'"

"Go get 'em, Pastor!" Zig would say with a laugh nearly every Sunday morning. "The Redhead"—his term of endearment for his beloved wife, Jean—"and I are cheering you on."

I could go on and on, because so many people have encouraged me through the years. I wonder, is it the same for you?

I wonder who your spiritual heroes are, the women and men who have left this earth but who linger in your heart and mind. A parent, perhaps, or a pastor? An older sibling? An elderly neighbor who took you in like a child of her own? Who comes to mind when you think of that beautiful band of witnesses cheering you forward every day of your life? Whose help do you covet as you face ordeals in this world? Whose faithfulness might spur you on?

One of the reasons I love helping people to reignite their faith is because when they do so, they tap into latent support they barely remember was there. "Heaven surrounds you and encompasses you!" I tell them and tell you now. "Heaven is unseen people eager to lend us a helping hand."

Heaven also is unseen power, as evidenced by God's omnipotence in *every* realm.

Heaven Is Unseen Power

To set the tone for this next part of the conversation, let's begin here: We serve an omnipotent God. Colossians 1:16 says, "For by him [God] all things were created, in heaven and on earth, visible and invisible, whether thrones or dominions or rulers or authorities—all things were created through him and for him."

What's more, we serve a God who does not change. "Every good gift and every perfect gift is from above," we read in James 1:17, "coming down from the Father of lights with whom there is no variation or shadow due to change."

Putting these two concepts together, we see that God is all-powerful, all the time. This means that even the deviance and destructiveness of those who plot evil in this world cannot thwart the power that is his alone.

In Ephesians 6, when the apostle Paul counsels believers at Ephesus to "be strong in the Lord," he does so because he recognizes what anyone paying attention can see: We are in a battle, and to neglect to look to God for power is to be vulnerable to attack. "Put on the whole armor of God," he says, "that you may be able to stand against the schemes of the devil. For we do not wrestle against flesh and blood, but against the rulers, against the authorities, against the cosmic powers over this present darkness, against the spiritual forces of evil in the heavenly places" (vv. 10–12).

This war is taking place in the *unseen realm*, in other words, which means we need *unseen power* to prevail. Like me, you've probably come away from a quick scroll through the news headlines, wondering, *How bad is this thing going to get?* There is economic recession, there is rampant job loss, there is terrorist activity on six continents, there are abortions, and hate crimes, and theft. There is cyberbullying. There is teen suicide. There is the sale of human body parts. There is sex trafficking. There is domestic abuse. There is *evil* at every turn, and if you and I didn't know that victory was assured in the end, we would lose heart and die of despair.

Thankfully, heaven's reality steps in and reminds us, *This life you're living here on earth isn't all there is.*

During Jesus' time on earth, he made some seemingly outlandish statements. For example, once he said to his disciples, "I am the way, and the truth, and the life. No one comes to the Father except through me" (John 14:6). This was radical thinking for the times . . . there's only *one* way to get to God?

Another time, Jesus said that he and the Father were "one" (John 10:30). Huh? Jesus thought he was *God*?

But perhaps the most outlandish of all the things to come out of Jesus' mouth was what he said at the funeral of a friend.

The man Lazarus had fallen ill, so Lazarus's sisters sent word to Jesus, alerting him to the problem on their hands. To their shock, it took Jesus three days to show up, even though he was less than a day's journey away. But eventually he made his way to the sisters, which is when he learned that Lazarus had died. Let's pick up the story there. In John 11, we read the following:

> Now when Jesus came, he found that Lazarus had already been in the tomb four days. Bethany was near Jerusalem, about two miles off, and many of the Jews had come to Martha and Mary

to console them concerning their brother. So when Martha heard that Jesus was coming, she went and met him, but Mary remained seated in the house. Martha said to Jesus, "Lord, if you had been here, my brother would not have died. But even now I know that whatever you ask from God, God will give you." Jesus said to her, "Your brother will rise again." Martha said to him, "I know that he will rise again in the resurrection on the last day."

vv. 17–24

And then came the bold statement from our Lord: "I am the resurrection and the life," he said to Martha. He wasn't just *able to resurrect*; no, what Jesus was saying was that he himself is resurrection itself. He—Jesus, God incarnate—*is* rebirth. He—Jesus, God incarnate—*is* new life. Forever life. Eternal life. Life that never sees death.

"Whoever believes in me," he continues, "though he die, yet shall he live, and everyone who lives and believes in me shall never die" (v. 25–26). Such a claim might have been considered lunacy were it not for the fact that Jesus then raised Lazarus from the dead. "He was just sleeping," Jesus had essentially said to his disciples. If the sisters heard about this comment, it must have taken them aback. *What was it that we smelled for four days?* they had to have wondered. *We know our brother was dead!*

In the mid-1920s, playwright Eugene O'Neill wrote the play *Lazarus Laughed*, a fictional accounting of this story in which the main character, Lazarus, returns from the dead to tell onlookers that there is, in fact, no death, but instead only God's eternal laughter. In an odd turn of events, the more Lazarus laughs after returning to life, the younger and stronger he becomes.

In the play, Lazarus can't keep quiet about being raised from the dead, but people aren't quite as enthusiastic about things as he. He goes to city after city, telling Romans, Jews, and Greeks his story and is met with hatred and death threats each time. What does Lazarus do in response?

You guessed it: Lazarus laughs.

Lazarus laughed because death had no hold over him; he'd been there and made it back. And he laughed because Jesus' power would protect him from any harm he might face. "To be absent from the body" is to be "present with the Lord," 2 Corinthians 5:8 (NKJV) reminds us, which means that while we may lose heart from time to time over the state of affairs in our lives and in our world, the presence of heaven beckons us forth: *This life isn't all there is.*

It should come as no surprise that in his letter to the Philippian church, the apostle Paul said that above all other things, he wanted to know the power of Jesus' resurrection. "Indeed, I count everything as loss because of the surpassing worth of knowing Christ Jesus my Lord," he writes in Philippians 3:8–11. "For his sake I have suffered the loss of all things and count them as rubbish, in order that I may gain Christ and be found in him, not having a righteousness of my own that comes from the law, but that which comes through faith in Christ, the righteousness from God that depends on faith—that I may know him and the power of his resurrection, and may share his sufferings, becoming like him in his death, that by any means possible I may attain the resurrection from the dead."

The thing that strikes me about Paul's sentiment is that this is *Paul* talking, the same man who endured more personal atrocities than you and I likely could imagine: "Five times I received at the hands of the Jews the forty lashes less one," he writes in 2 Corinthians 11:24–28. (Thirty-nine lashes of a whip was the legal limit then.) "Three times I was beaten with rods. Once I was stoned. Three times I was shipwrecked; a night and a day I was adrift at sea; on frequent journeys, in danger from rivers, danger from robbers, danger from my own people, danger from Gentiles, danger in the city, danger in the wilderness, danger at sea, danger from false brothers; in toil and hardship, through many a sleepless night, in hunger and thirst, often without food, in cold and exposure. And, apart from other things, there is the daily pressure on me of my anxiety for all the churches."

Were that my unreasonable résumé, I might ask for recompense. For reparations. For justice to be served. But what Paul realized is that every earthly resource we might long for bends its knee to the power of Christ. As it relates to the power of Jesus' resurrection, Paul's plea implies, what else could possibly matter if he has taken hold of that?

This ought to be instructive for you and me, because life can be ridiculously difficult, and grief is a very real thing. This power of Christ's resurrection? It is a balm for you and for me.

Thirteen months after my father was murdered, Deb's dad died of cancer. Deb and I were fatherless, twenty-year-old newlyweds who had to figure out fast whether we were going to thrive or cave. A verse from Paul's writings to the Corinthian church set our course. In what seemed to be part of Paul's greeting to the believers, he reminds them of a key aspect of who God is: "Blessed be the God and Father of our Lord Jesus Christ, the Father of mercies and God of all comfort, who comforts us in all our affliction, so that we may be able to comfort those who are in any affliction, with the comfort with which we ourselves are comforted by God. For as we share abundantly in Christ's sufferings, so through Christ we share abundantly in comfort too. If we are afflicted, it is for your comfort and salvation; and if we are comforted, it is for your comfort, which you experience when you patiently endure the same sufferings that we suffer. Our hope for you is unshaken, for we know that as you share in our sufferings, you will also share in our comfort" (2 Corinthians 1:3–7).

So much *comfort* in that passage—which is exactly what my new bride and I needed. But how, exactly, did the comforting work? We sat with the progression for months, until it planted itself in our hearts: God is a God of all comfort; God comforts us in our affliction with the comfort that's already ours in him; as we hurt in the same way that Jesus hurt, we gain access to the comfort that Jesus was comforted with; as those we know hurt in the same way that we hurt, they gain access to the comfort that we ourselves were comforted with.

You have surely known pain and heartache in this life, as have I. What this passage sealed in me was the belief that as we ache, we will be comforted *so that* as others ache, we can comfort them too.

An ancient Spanish proverb says, "There has never been a home without its hush," and in my pastoral experience, this assertion has proven true. Everyone I come across has poured out tears over *something*: the loss of a child or loved one, the loss of one's own health, the loss of a marriage, the loss of a career, the loss of a ministry. Deb's and my dear friend Cheri once said of her own grief over losing her husband to an affair and then to illness, "You cry until you can't cry anymore."

Millions of tears cried in my presence . . . billions, perhaps. In those moments in my office, in people's living rooms, in courtrooms, in jail cells, in hospital rooms, in nursing homes, in funeral homes, at gravesides, it seems there is no comfort to be found. Even then—especially then—God says, "If you will receive it, my comfort is here."

To know "the power of Jesus' resurrection" is to know that even in death, you can find comfort, let alone in life's circumstances that feel like death. My dear mother died not long after my dad was killed, and I've always wondered if she died of a broken heart. My whole family was reeling after Dad was gone, but Mom especially so. The pain, the shock, the agony, the loss—it was all too much to bear, and yet to this day I can't help but think, *What would have happened if instead of dying of a broken heart, Mom had been able to gather up her broken heart and live?*

Because we know that this world is not our final destination, we can set our grief in proper perspective and use our pain to help others pull through.

Whatever it is that you've overcome—addiction, infertility, disease—can be your ministry to the world. Another option exists besides turning inward and fading away; you can be comforted, you can be healed, you can be used for God's greater good.

"Blessed are you who mourn," Jesus said (see Matthew 5:4). After preaching about the depression I'd despised, and seeing the wild impact that candor had, I finally got what Jesus meant. To have my pain transformed into God's purpose . . . that's when the "blessing" came to me.

Several years ago, I watched the news in horror as reports flooded my feed about a twenty-six-year-old armed man who had walked into a Sunday-morning worship service in Sutherland Springs, Texas, three hundred miles south, and opened fire. In the eleven-minute rampage, Devin Kelley killed twenty-six people—ten women, seven men, seven girls, one boy, and an unborn child—making it the deadliest mass shooting in Texas history and the fifth deadliest in the United States. After a high-speed chase involving a church member who was legally carrying a firearm, Devin took his own life inside his SUV.

The following Monday, I phoned Pastor Frank Pomeroy—pastor at First Baptist Church Sutherland Springs, where the shooting had occurred—to offer my condolences. One of the girls who had been murdered was his fourteen-year-old daughter, Annabelle, and his grief was palpable as we talked. At one point, he said quietly, "Dr. Graham, I'm going to need to step away now, because they're asking me to come identify my daughter's body."

"Of course," I said, my heart in my throat. "I am so sorry for your incredible loss. . . ."

I disconnected the call and sat silently for some time. Such senseless tragedy . . . how was that dad supposed to go on? And yet in the days and weeks that followed, both Pastor Pomeroy and the entirety of his congregation declared that they'd do just that. "We will not give up!" they said through tears. "We will keep worship-ing! We will keep praying! We will keep serving as the Church! We will rise up, not give up!"

We will rise up, not give up.

We will rise up, not give up.

This is the power of Christ's resurrection, flowing through be-lievers in him. This world is not our home. *This isn't all there is.*

Heaven Is an Unseen Promise

But if this isn't all there is, what is left to come? Heaven is not only unseen people and unseen power but also an *unseen promise*. And while the Bible doesn't disclose the answers to all our questions regarding what our eternal home will be like, thankfully it does answer enough of them to assure us that it will be *good*.

Throughout the Bible—in 1,845 specific places, in fact—reference is made to the second coming of Jesus or to the eternal kingdom of God, which tells us that this event is eagerly antic-ipated, that it is cause for celebration, and that it is *real*. By way of example, we read in Job 19:25 that our "Redeemer lives, and at the last he will stand upon the earth." We read in Isaiah 9:6–7 that the Lord's name shall be called "Wonderful Counselor, Mighty God, Everlasting Father, Prince of Peace" and that "of the increase of his government and of peace there will be no end, on the throne of David and over his kingdom."

Jeremiah 23:5 says, "Behold, the days are coming, declares the Lord, when I will raise up for David a righteous Branch, and he shall reign as king and deal wisely, and shall execute justice and righteousness in the land."

Zechariah 14:3–4 says, "Then the Lord will go out and fight against those nations as when he fights on a day of battle. On that day his feet shall stand on the Mount of Olives that lies before Jerusalem on the east, and the Mount of Olives shall be split in two from east to west by a very wide valley, so that one half of the Mount shall move northward, and the other half southward."

One of my favorite experiences over the years has been leading trips to Israel, and one of my favorite parts of every trip is standing atop the Mount of Olives where you can enjoy a stunning panoramic view of the city of Jerusalem. On one side lies the garden of Gethsemane, where Jesus sweated drops of blood prior to his crucifixion, and on the other side are the locales where Jesus taught people about who he was and why he'd come. The Bible says that at his second coming, Jesus will stand on that mountain, and a great earthquake will split the place in two. What a sight that will be! "For the Lord himself will descend from heaven with a cry of command," Paul says in 1 Thessalonians 4:16–18, "with the voice of an archangel, and with the sound of the trumpet of God. And the dead in Christ will rise first. Then we who are alive, who are left, will be caught up together with them in the clouds to meet the Lord in the air, and so we will always be with the Lord. Therefore encourage one another with these words."

Jesus is coming back. And it won't be a subtle event. In Matthew 24:40–41, we read, "Then two men will be in the field; one will be taken and one left. Two women will be grinding at the mill; one will be taken and one left." Following this rapture of the Church comes the retribution of the earth: "And then the lawless one will be revealed," Paul writes in 2 Thessalonians 2:8–9, "whom the Lord Jesus will kill with the breath of his mouth and bring to nothing by the appearance of his coming. The coming of the lawless one is by the activity of Satan with all power and false signs and wonders."

The rapture, the retribution, the revelation of the antichrist, and then, finally, the return of Jesus Christ in all his glory on the earth. "Then the seventh angel blew his trumpet, and there were loud voices in heaven, saying, 'The kingdom of the world has become the kingdom of our Lord and of his Christ, and he shall reign forever and ever'" (Revelation 11:15). Amen and hallelujah!

Now, I bring all this up because once we understand what is coming our way, we have a place to put what is here. When a baby is about to be born, I'm told, the labor pains are easier to bear. And oh, the labor pains we are seeing today! There are *moral* pains: "Lawlessness will be increased," we're told in Matthew 24:12, and "the love of many will grow cold." There are *political* pains: "For nation will rise against nation," Matthew 24:7 reports, "and kingdom against kingdom, and there will be famines and earthquakes in various places." There are *spiritual* pains: "For false christs and false prophets will arise and perform great signs and wonders, so as to lead astray, if possible, even the elect" (Matthew 24:24).

Without question, these are tough times for us all—even dangerous, perilous times. But put into proper perspective, these times can point us to their culmination in Christ. "We are God's children now," John writes, "and what we will be has not yet appeared; but we know that when he appears we shall be like him, because we shall see him as he is" (1 John 3:2).

We need not let our hearts be troubled, John says in John 14:1. We believe in God. Now, we can believe in Christ. And to believe in Christ is to believe Christ, who says that a place is being prepared—"many mansions," Jesus says. We will not always know devastation, in other words. We will not always know despair. This existence we're merely passing through is leading us beautifully *home*.

"The road leads home," one songwriter said. "Who could mind the journey when the road leads home?"[4]

"You also, be patient," says James in James 5:8. "Establish your hearts, for the coming of the Lord is at hand."

Establish your hearts, for the coming of the Lord is at hand— this is the central invitation of Christ. "If then you have been raised with Christ," Paul says in Colossians 3:1–4, "seek the things that are above, where Christ is, seated at the right hand of God.

Set your minds on things that are above, not on things that are on earth. For you have died, and your life is hidden with Christ in God. When Christ who is your life appears, then you also will appear with him in glory."

Seek not after what is here in this life, but rather what will be in the life to come.

Seek not after only what you see with your eyes, but rather what exists in the unseen realm.

Seek not after all that will one day slip away, but rather what will last, and stand, and live on.

Let it be said of you, by those looking back, "Now *that* was a person of faith."

Acknowledgments

A book is not a solo project. It is the creation of multiple people, influences, and life experiences. I am deeply grateful to all who have encouraged me to write this book, especially Ashley Wiersma, who has now collaborated with me on four books. She transforms my words into paragraphs and pages and captures the voice of this author with ease.

To my friends at Bethany House, especially Andy McGuire, my great encourager.

To my dear friend and book agent, Robert Wolgemuth, who is a consummate professional and a beloved prayer partner.

To the great people of Prestonwood Baptist Church, who have allowed me to be their pastor for thirty-one years and counting. I am privileged each week to deliver God's Word to the finest congregation on earth.

To Deb Graham, my wife of fifty years. We were college sweethearts and after a lifetime of serving Christ together find ourselves still very much in love. She is a gift to me from God.

To my Savior and Lord, always and forever. My life, my all, is for Him. All the praise goes to Jesus.

Notes

Chapter 1: Truth That Never Turns

1. Tim Clinton, Archibald Hart, and George Ohlschlager, *Caring for People God's Way: Personal and Emotional Issues, Addictions, Grief, and Trauma* (Nashville, TN: Thomas Nelson, 2005), 144.

2. Clinton, Hart, and Ohlschlager, *Caring for People God's Way*, 146.

3. Haruki Murakami, *What I Talk About When I Talk About Running: A Memoir* (New York: Penguin Random House, 2008), 64.

4. Ed Dobson, *Seeing through the Fog: Hope When Your World Falls Apart* (Colorado Springs, CO: David C. Cook, 2012), 70.

5. Stephanie Lobdell, *Signs of Life: Resurrecting Hope Out of Ordinary Losses* (Harrisonburg, VA: Herald Press, 2019), 44.

6. See 1 Samuel 28.

7. "A Christian Looks at Depression - Tommy Nelson," Dallas Theological Seminary, May 8, 2012, video, https://www.youtube.com/watch?v=jXecSlwVBTQ&feature=emb_logo&ab_channel=DallasTheologicalSeminary.

8. Kristen Welch, *Made to Move Mountains: How God Uses Our Dreams and Disasters to Accomplish the Impossible* (Grand Rapids, MI: Baker Books, 2020), 105.

9. Jerry A. Gladson, *For God's Sake, Do Something!: Selected Sermons from the Old Testament* (New York: Writers Club Press, 2003), 122.

10. I adapted this list from something I came across in John F. Walvoord's revision of Lewis Sperry Chafer's marvelous book, *Major Bible Themes: 52 Vital Doctrines of the Scriptures Simplified and Explained*, published by Zondervan in 1926 and 1953. If you haven't yet read this one, I highly encourage you to do so.

11. Clinton, Hart, and Ohlschlager, 144.

12. Dr. Paul Brand and Philip Yancey, *Fearfully and Wonderfully: The Marvel of Bearing God's Image*, updated and combined ed., (Downers Grove, IL: IVP Books, 2019), 173.

13. Dr. Marc Brackett, *Permission to Feel: The Power of Emotional Intelligence to Achieve Well-Being and Success* (New York: Celadon Books, 2019), 105.

14. Kay Arthur, *How to Study Your Bible: The Lasting Rewards of the Inductive Approach* (Eugene, OR: Harvest House Publishers, 1994), 139.

15. Karen Swallow Prior, *On Reading Well: Finding the Good Life through Great Books* (Grand Rapids, MI: Brazos Press, 2018), 17.

16. Robert Morgan, *Reclaiming the Lost Art of Biblical Meditation: Find True Peace in Jesus* (Nashville: HarperCollins, 2017), xi.

17. Charles H. Spurgeon, *Letters to My Students* (Classic Christian eBooks), 173.

Chapter 2: Prayer That Never Fails

1. "What Is Stress?" the American Institute of Stress, accessed October 13, 2020, https://www.stress.org/what-is-stress.

2. "42 Worrying Workplace Stress Statistics," the American Institute of Stress, September 25, 2019, https://www.stress.org/42-worrying-workplace-stress-statistics.

3. "What Is Stress?" the American Institute of Stress, accessed October 13, 2020, https://www.stress.org/daily-life/.

4. "America's #1 Health Problem," the American Institute of Stress, accessed October 13, 2020, https://www.stress.org/americas-1-health-problem.

5. Charles Spurgeon, "The Raven's Cry," sermon at Metropolitan Tabernacle, January 14, 1866, https://www.ccel.org/ccel/spurgeon/sermons12.v.html.

6. I'm deviating a bit from Adrian's original description, using the word *commit* rather than *control*.

7. Warren W. Wiersbe, *Wiersbe's Expository Outlines on the Old Testament: Strategic Chapters Outlined, Explained, and Practically Applied* (Colorado Springs, CO: Victor, 1993), 411.

Chapter 3: Loving What Jesus Loves

1. Eugene Peterson, *Practice Resurrection: A Conversation on Growing Up in Christ* (Grand Rapids, MI: William B. Eerdmans Publishing, 2010), 12.

2. Conrad Hackett and David McClendon, "Christians remain world's largest religious group, but they are declining in Europe," Pew Research Center, April 5, 2017, https://www.pewresearch.org/fact-tank/2017/04/05/christians-remain-worlds-largest-religious-group-but-they-are-declining-in-europe/.

3. Erin Duffin, "Church attendance of Americans 2019," Statista, January 17, 2020, https://www.statista.com/statistics/245491/church-attendance-of-americans/.

4. Justin Whitmel Earley, *The Common Rule: Habits of Purpose for an Age of Distraction* (Downers Grove, IL: IVP Books, 2019), 49.

5. Vivek H. Murthy, *Together: The Healing Power of Human Connection in a Sometimes Lonely World* (New York: HarperCollins, 2020), xiii.

6. Murthy, *Together*, xix.

7. Julianne Holt-Lunstad, Timothy B. Smith, "Loneliness and social isolation as risk factors for CVD: implications for evidence-based patient care and scientific inquiry," *BMJ Journals: Heart* 102, no. 13 (2016): 987–989.

8. John T. Cacioppo and Stephanie Cacioppo, "The Growing Problem of Loneliness," *The Lancet* 391, no. 10119 (February 3, 2018): 426, https://www.thelancet.com/journals/lancet/article/PIIS0140-6736(18)30142-9/fulltext.

Chapter 4: Living from Victory

1. "Elephant Herd Protects Their Baby from Lions | Serengeti," Discovery, August 5, 2019, video, https://www.youtube.com/watch?v=lNfjjjgq3Hs.

2. "You 2.0: Why We're Bad at Predicting Our Own Happiness — And How We Can Get Better," *Hidden Brain*, NPR, August 21, 2017, https://www.npr.org/transcripts/545097480.

3. "You 2.0," *Hidden Brain*, https://www.npr.org/transcripts/545097480.

4. Max Lucado, *Fearless: Imagine Your Life Without Fear* (Nashville: Thomas Nelson, 2009), 5.

5. Jen Pollock Michel, *Surprised by Paradox: The Promise of And in an Either-Or World* (Downers Grove, IL: IVP Books, 2019), 167.

6. See James 4:7.

Chapter 5: Exchanging Doubt for Faith

1. Megan Davies and Walden Siew, "45 Percent of World's Wealth Destroyed: Blackstone CEO," Reuters, March 10, 2009, https://www.reuters.com/article/us-blackstone-idUSTRE52966Z20090310.

2. "The World's Billionaires," Forbes, March 11, 2009, https://www.forbes.com/2009/03/11/worlds-richest-people-billionaires-2009-billionaires-intro.html#705aeff53847.

3. Andrew Soergel, "Fed Official Warns of 30% Unemployment," U.S. News & World Report, March 23, 2020, https://www.usnews.com/news/economy/articles/2020-03-23/fed-official-unemployment-could-hit-30-as-coronavirus-slams-economy.

4. "Key Statistics & Graphics," Economic Research Service, United States Department of Agriculture, updated September 9, 2020, https://www.ers.usda.gov/topics/food-nutrition-assistance/food-security-in-the-us/key-statistics-graphics.aspx#.

5. Max Roser and Hannah Ritchie, "Hunger and Undernourishment," OurWorldInData.org, 2013, https://ourworldindata.org/hunger-and-undernourishment#.

6. Sejal Kapadia Pocha, "J. K. Rowling Offers Touching Advice to a Fan Suffering Depression," *Stylist*, accessed October 13, 2020, https://www.stylist.co.uk/people/j-k-rowling-gives-touching-advice-to-a-fan-suffering-depression-anxiety/27011.

7. Jerry Bridges, *The Practice of Godliness* (Colorado Springs, CO: NavPress, 1983), 147.

8. Bridges, *The Practice of Godliness*, 147.

Chapter 6: Exchanging Discontentment for Gratitude

1. Grace Gold, "This Is the Age When You Start to Visibly Look Older," *Marie Claire*, November 3, 2015, https://www.marieclaire.com/beauty/news/a16636/the-age-when-aging-begins/.

2. Amy Morin, "7 Scientifically Proven Benefits of Gratitude That Will Motivate You to Give Thanks Year-Round," *Forbes*, November 23, 2014, https://www.forbes.com/sites/amymorin/2014/11/23/7-scientifically-proven-benefits-of-gratitude-that-will-motivate-you-to-give-thanks-year-round/.

3. "Ruth Bell Graham's 5 Truths on Prodigals and Those Who Love Them," Billy Graham Evangelistic Association, April 21, 2016, https://billygraham.org/story/ruth-bell-grahams-5-truths-on-prodigals-and-those-who-love-them/.

4. McDaniel, *In Want + Plenty*, 209–210.

5. "Thank You, Lord (for Saving My Soul)," Seth and Bessie Sykes, Singspiration Music, 1968.

Chapter 7: Exchanging Distress for Peace

1. "How Many Wars Are Going on in the World Right Now?" Reference.com, updated April 1, 2020, reference.com/world-view/many-wars-going-world-right-now-ffd6236450ccb7ae.

2. Horatio Spafford, "When Peace, Like a River," 1873.

3. Charles Swindoll, *Living the Proverbs: Insights for the Daily Grind* (Brentwood, Tennessee: Worthy Publishing, 2012), 48.

4. Collin Hansen, "Top 10 Most-Searched Bible Verses: What's Missing?" January 23, 2011, https://www.thegospelcoalition.org/article/top-10-most-searched-bible-verses-whats-missing/.

Chapter 8: Wanting What God Wants

1. Attributed to Jean-Paul Sartre in Jim Kwik, *Limitless: Upgrade Your Brain, Learn Anything Faster, and Unlock Your Exceptional Life* (Carlsbad, CA: Hay House, 2020), 54.

2. Holly Dunsworth, "Monkeys All the Way Down," *Sapiens*, January 28, 2016, https://www.sapiens.org/column/origins/monkeys-all-the-way-down/.

3. *The Confessions of St. Augustine, Bishop of Hippo*, trans. J. G. Pilkington (Edinburgh: T. & T. Clark, 1876), 1.

4. George Albert Shepperson, "David Livingstone," Britannica, accessed October 13, 2020, https://www.britannica.com/biography/David-Livingstone/Influence.

5. Westminster Shorter Catechism, https://ccel.org/ccel/anonymous/westminster1/westminster1.i.i.html.

6. John H. Sammis, "When We Walk with the Lord," 1887.

7. Sam Parker and Mac Anderson, *212 The Extra Degree: Extraordinary Results Begin with One Small Change* (Naperville, IL: Sourcebooks, 2018), 9.

8. Jen Pollock Michel, *Surprised by Paradox: The Promise of And in an Either-Or World* (Downers Grove, IL: IVP Books, 2019), 68.

Chapter 9: Giving Good Gifts

1. James Rowe, "Love Lifted Me," 1912.

2. Rebecca McLaughlin, *Confronting Christianity: 12 Hard Questions for the World's Largest Religion* (Wheaton, IL: Crossway Books, 2019), 31.

Chapter 10: And So, We Begin Again

1. "December 9, 1914: Edison Sees His Vast Plant Burn," *This Week in New Jersey History*, December 8, 2008, https://njhistory.wordpress.com/2008/12/08/hello-world/.

2. Seth Slater, "Can Smiling Make Us Happy?" *Psychology Today*, March 27, 2014, https://www.psychologytoday.com/us/blog/the-dolphin-divide/201403/can-smiling-make-us-happy.

3. Jon Gordon (@JonGordon11), Twitter, December 22, 2016, https://twitter.com/JonGordon11/status/812080762744897536.

4. St. Patrick, "Deer's Cry," in Newport J. D. White, St Patrick: His Writings and Life (New York: The Macmillan Company, 1920), 64–67.

Chapter 11: Gaze Set on Things Unseen

1. For more, see *Angels: Who They Are, What They Do, and Why It Matters* (Minneapolis: Bethany House, 2016).

2. Zig Ziglar, *Over the Top: Moving from Survival to Stability, from Stability to Success, from Success to Significance*, rev. and updated ed. (Nashville: Thomas Nelson, 1997), 48.

3. Ziglar, *Over the Top*, 194.

4. James M. Gray, "The Road Leads Home."

About the Author

Dr. Jack Graham is pastor of Prestonwood Baptist Church, one of the nation's largest, most dynamic congregations with more than 47,000 members. He is the acclaimed author of *Angels: Who They Are, What They Do, and Why It Matters*, as well as numerous other books, and his passionate, biblical teaching can be viewed and heard across the globe via PowerPoint Ministries. Through broadcasts and online sermons, he addresses everyday issues prevalent in today's culture that strike a chord with audiences everywhere.

Dr. Graham was honorary chairman of the 2015 National Day of Prayer, and he twice served as president of the Southern Baptist Convention, the largest Protestant denomination in the U.S. He was ordained to the gospel ministry in 1970 and holds a master of divinity degree with honors and a doctor of ministry degree in church and proclamation from Southwestern Baptist Theological Seminary. He and his wife, Deb, have three grown children and eight grandchildren.

Learn more about Dr. Graham and view a complete list of his books at www.jackgraham.org.

More from Jack Graham

 BETHANYHOUSE